REAL LIFE TRADING™ PSYCHOLOGY

MASTER YOURSELF,
MASTER
THE MARKETS

FINDING INTERNAL GREATNESS
AND FINANCIAL FREEDOM

JERREMY ALEXANDER NEWSOME

Master Yourself, Master the Markets:
Finding Internal Greatness and Financial Freedom

www.jerremynewsome.com
www.reallifetrading.com

Published by Made to Change the World™ Publishing
Nashville, Tennessee

Cover and interior designed by Chelsea Jewell

Paperback ISBN: 978-1-956837-30-8
Ebook ISBN: 978-1-956837-31-5

Printed in the USA, Canada, Australia, and Europe

To my family. Relationships are our truest form of wealth. It was an honor to travel the United States in an RV with you, chipping away at this book in the cool air of the 6:00 am mornings, parked in the most glorious spots our national parks have to offer. Thank you Svetlana, Gabriel, Json, and future baby boy for giving me peace, happiness, serenity, and a fuel that is never ending as I journey continuously into my purpose.

And to you:

- The dreamer and the doer.

- The fifty-year-old nurse who is tired of being told what to do and when to do it.

- The overworked, underpaid teacher who spends your own money to ensure your students have the right resources to learn as you teach them for sixty-plus hours a week.

- The engineer who loves patterns, numbers, certainty, and math-based rules.

- The spouse who dreams of taking a three-week vacation once a year with all of your family.

This book is for you.

Within these pages, may you discover your path to wealth creation and true liberation.

Let's goooooooooooooooooooooooooooooooo!

CONTENTS

Social media allows us to connect with people in our industry better than anytime in the past. As a stock trader, I find X (formerly Twitter) to be a very valuable resource. To learn new strategies and ideas, I follow a number of successful traders, including Jerremy Newsome (@newsomenuggets). I follow a lot of traders on X, but Jerremy is different. Not only is he a good trader, he is unrelentingly positive, always posting something inspirational and uplifting. Because there are always ups and downs in trading, I find Jerremy's posts to be very refreshing, especially when I'm on a cold streak.

In 2018, I was heading to Nashville. Knowing Jerremy was from there, I reached out to him to see if he was free for lunch. I sent him a DM on X, and he responded almost instantaneously with an enthusiastic, "YES my man!!" We exchanged numbers and agreed to meet. A few minutes after making the lunch arrangements, I got a text from Jerremy, "This is going to be incredible!!" I didn't know if he was referring to the food at the restaurant or if he was really that excited for our meeting. Not knowing how to respond, I just said, "For sure."

The next day, another text from Jerremy, "I'm so excited, this meeting is going to be phenomenal." The text made me smile and chuckle. I'm the one who reached out to him, but he was more excited than me!

One last text message, the morning of our meeting, "This is going to be stupendous!" After googling the word "stupendous," I thought to myself, "He may be setting the bar a little bit too high for this meeting." I texted him back, "Looking forward to it."

When he entered the restaurant, he walked over and gave me a huge hug like he had known me his whole life. That's who Jerremy is. When he does something, he's all in, giving 110 percent even to a simple lunch meeting with a person he's never met.

We sat down and started talking about stocks that we liked, but the conversation quickly turned toward stock charts. I like charts and have always respected technical analysis, but it has never been the focus of my trading. So when Jerremy mentioned charts, I thought to myself, "Here we go, another retail trader selling me on the next head and shoulders or cup and handle pattern." But Jerremy approached them in a whole different way. He talked about day traders being trapped and needing to cover. He was looking at failed breakouts. He was actually going against many traditional technical strategies that you would read in a textbook. I was intrigued. "Go on," I said.

He discussed pattern recognition and identifying opportunities on both the long and the short side. Most traders on X are long only (meaning they don't play the short side, or, if they do, it's by buying puts—not outright shorting stocks). I quickly realized that I was in the company of one of the most sophisticated traders that I had ever met. And he was coming up with these strategies and conclusions by looking at simple candlestick patterns! I picked his brain for another thirty minutes, and we wrapped up lunch with another hug. I've been good friends with him ever since.

After knowing Jerremy for the past five years, I can tell you that he has a very unique style of trading. He looks at candlestick charts in a simple but elegant way, which allows him to profit in all market conditions, not just bull markets. You will find many of these trading strategies in the second half of this book.

Jerremy has a deep understanding of trader psychology, which allows him to effectively coach and mentor new and struggling traders. Trading is all about confidence. The most successful traders know how to control their emotions to minimize their mental damage during losing streaks and maximize their potential gains when trading is going well. A confident trader doesn't hesitate. They strike quickly when they identify the setup they are looking for, and they exit quickly when the trade is not working out.

This brings me to the number one reason Jerremy has been successful in this industry—his focus on discipline. Discipline is the key to any successful trading strategy. If you cut your winners too short or hold onto your losers too long, you are doomed to fail.

Jerremy has developed a system of risk management called the R system. It allows traders to quantify the risk and reward on every trade before ever making the trade. This way, they don't overtrade and only take the cleanest setups. If you swing at every pitch, you're bound to strike out.

The best traders find a way to keep their trading strategies fresh and simple. They have a firm understanding of the core principles and know how to keep their emotions in check. If you're new to trading or struggling to find your edge, this book will be a valuable resource for identifying and developing your own trading edge. The key is to give 110 percent like Jerremy does, and you'll have the best chance of finding success. Good luck, and enjoy learning from one of the best.

—Dennis Dick

ACKNOWLEDGMENTS

I find inspiration through my daily devotion of always seeking truth, enrichment, education, and guidance.

Jen Sincero, we haven't worked together *yet*, but thank you for giving me permission to write however I want.

Emily Young, thank you for sending me daily motivational messages that allowed me to see greatness within myself.

Gisela Sanchez-Vaynshteyn, thank you for attending almost every event, trip, and program that I ever created.

The synapses in my brain and the neural pathways along with core memories were created because of the following individuals: Tony Robbins, Joe Dispenza, Michael Beckwith, Earl Nightingale, Alan Watts, Jordan Peterson, Joe Rogan, Jesse Itzler, Brené Brown, Colin O'Brady, T.D. Jakes, Billy Alsbrooks, Jim Rohn, Zig Ziglar, Les Brown, Eric Thomas, Britnie Turner, Preston Brown, Chuck Hogan, Dean Inniss, Alex Hormozi, Zach Homol. It has been an honor to stand on your shoulders, learn from your wisdom and teachings, obtain guidance and information from your embodied greatness, and pour into others my energy, zeal, and enthusiasm that is unmatched for education and enrichment!

To my Real Life Trading family, what a journey. I had no clue that a dirt-poor boy from Georgia would ever be capable of feeling such love and admiration! Together, we've traveled with our families all over the world, trading alongside each other on the beach, on park benches, on disk-golf courses, and in the nicest hotel lobbies this world has to offer. I've found a home in the arms of everyone who cared for me so dearly at my baby start-up that turned into a household name—thank you!

Monumental thanks to Libby Pease who changed my entire world in 2019 by guiding me to sobriety, helping me see my future so brightly, and asking questions that no one else would ever dare to ask, propelling me into a new atmosphere of accomplishment.

Judy Potter, with no relation to Harry, is one of the most magnificent healers on this planet. She ripped my soul apart and put it back together in McCaysville, Georgia.

And, of course, to my Queen, my savior, my bride, my everything, Svetlana. I never thought I would be satisfied and satiated, truly complete, whole and happy until you came into my life. Thank you for being my missing puzzle piece.

INTRODUCTION

Why did I write this book?

I cannot recall a time, a moment in my life, where I did not have this fierce internal fire, this hunger ... not for food, but for mental liberation of those around me.

Imagine running for hours in the hottest temperatures possible. You know that thirst? That dry mouth? That "When I get water, I will be joyously refreshed" feeling?? That is how my brain and body feel when I know something that others probably do not.

It is my purpose—call it a mission—to provide to you the level of happiness, energy, and conviction that I feel each and every day.

And I earn that happiness, energy, and conviction by trading in the stock market. It has saved my life.

The stock market is like an ocean. It's constructed of waves on top of waves; the smaller waves destined to become bigger waves that change the landscape of the surrounding continents. It's that awesome.

But it has baffled individuals for decades, creating a firestorm of hysteria that keeps people awake at night. It can even morph into a fiscal thief that robs willing participants of their thoughts during the day.

The stock market is a velociraptor hiding in the tall grass waiting for you to be impatient.

But, for disciplined traders, the stock market is like your kind grandparent who lovingly assembles your favorite PB&J sandwich cut into three equal-sized pieces and gives it to you with your choco-milk but only after you have done your chores.

My greatest gift, my most honed superpower, is taking a complex subject—trading—and distilling it down into easy, motivational, and almost annoyingly oversimplified mental morsels.

So let me be your guide! I will remove for you all of the harmful mind grenades and trip wires while carefully providing the most exciting and valuable book on the psychology of the markets.

If you read this book in its entirety, you will know what I know about the stock market; you will receive fifteen years of experience along with your doctorate of "what not to do."

As you complete each chapter, you will finally feel, see, and understand how easy the path to wealth is.

This book will change your trading and, thus, your life. Read it with care and precision. Visit its bespoke chapters when you feel the need arise, and know that as long as the internet works, I will be here to guide you and your family to financial freedom using the stock market as my vehicle of choice!

CHAPTER 1 :
MASTER YOURSELF AND YOU WILL MASTER THE MARKETS

"I no longer play small; I want to serve the world; I want to liberate others from fear, from depression; my mission in life is to enrich lives with mentally liberating education; that is why I am here, that is my calling."
—Jerremy Alexander Newsome

Can any one person truly master themselves? What does it even mean to master oneself? How does one do it, and why does one need to? For me, true mastery of the inner self sounded vague and unobtainable. And I didn't understand the relevance that self-mastery had to becoming a full-time, profitable trader anyway.

Over many years, I came to appreciate that to become better at anything outside myself, I needed to become better within myself. The notion that *our outer wealth will never exceed our inner wealth* clicked, and I knew I needed to share that deep insight with anyone who is seeking to trade as a profession.

For the last decade, I've had the honor of working with tens of thousands of clients all looking for ways to improve who they are and what they do. We've worked one-on-one, in-person, online, in group mentorships, and in seminars, webinars, podcasts, lectures, and events. These men and women of all ages, income levels, backgrounds, religions, spiritual beliefs, monetary considerations, and diverse trading styles have all been met with the same admiration and simultaneous disdain by the liquid markets.

This book is intended to be the Holy Grail of trader psychology, written by a trader, for traders. My hope is that it will be your go-to resource whenever you are stuck, on a losing streak, or have anxiety as it relates to growth and success. I'll share my losses, my wins, and my personal reflections.

Whether you trade bonds, commodities, cryptocurrencies, forex, futures, options, stocks, warrants, or even baseball cards, this book will give you the needed insights to *master yourself and master the markets*. It is your manual for internal greatness and your guide to financial freedom.

My first tip: Finish the book! Let me repeat, finish the book! If you start and do not finish, you have zero chance of achieving the financial success you think you deserve.

Zero percent. Or in trading terms, zero R. *More on this soon.* Always commit to finishing what you start. This will become the cornerstone of your discipline and success!

Discipline is a main topic of this book, and, if you can master it, it will bring you closer to mastering yourself.

The chapters here are short, sweet, and simple; they offer sound advice while giving you small doses of victory as you soar through each one!

Are you ready to seek greatness and success while simultaneously leaning into the peace and harmony within yourself?

It is time for you to strip away the layers that are holding you back from your own excellence.

It is time to *master yourself and master the markets.* LET'S GO!!

CHAPTER 2 :
MASTER TIME AND YOU WILL MASTER THE MARKETS

"I don't have the time." Is this the most common excuse in the world? I hear it everyday. You hear it everyday ...

The *feeling* of being crunched for time is the number one cause of stress. And everyone wants to alleviate that stress by making more money, which eventually becomes the all-consuming mental hamster wheel.

But time can't be owned or possessed. There is an endless supply of books written about time management and a plethora of articles discussing the scientific construct of time and its boundless existence. From an awareness perspective, time does not exist. Humans created time and its measurements in the name of structuring life and society.

You need time to work, prepare, eat meals, and partake in meditations, yoga, or exercise for your health and spiritual intentions.

Somewhere in there, you also need to squeeze in time for reading a book, running over to Mom's, staying in touch with friends, expanding your mind, learning something new, cleaning the dishes, food shopping, doctor visits ... Have I mentioned the laundry yet? And let's not forget, at some point, you have to sleep and work, right?

So how do you do it all? Through time management. Value your time, know what you are worth, and schedule all appointments on your personal calendar. It's that simple. Knowing how to effectively manage time to master it is exactly why I have written this book.

"Rich people have money; wealthy people have time!"
—Shane Parrish

At its highest level, success is making and completing priorities and necessary tasks while reaping the benefits of doing so. This book is not about telling you the importance of creating priorities. You've already heard that a million times.

This book is about offering you practical guidance, pointers, and mindset hacks that will free you from life's stressors related to the construct of time so that you can prioritize what will ultimately lead you to self-mastery and success.

As part of that practical and tactical guidance, let's start with a straight-forward calculation to determine your daily time value. Do this to ensure your understanding of the costs and value of your time!

By creating your time value per waking hour, you'll learn to value your time more effectively and efficiently. First, take the total amount of money, the gross, pre-tax dollar amount, you made in the last calendar year. Divide it by 365 (days of the year), and then divide that number by 24 (hours). See the example:

$145,304	Gross, Pre-Tax Dollar Amount on Currency Units, Realized Gains for the Last Calendar Year
$145,304/365	$398.09
$398.09/24	$16.59
Your Hourly Life Value	$16.59

What this number reveals is twofold. First, it tells you how much you're worth per hour of your life. Second, it brings your time-life value to your awareness so you can use this number to attribute to your daily tasks.

Let me explain. Using the above example, let's assume you spend three hours a week grocery shopping. Multiply those three hours by your hourly life value of $16.59, and you used $49.77 worth of time-life value units on shopping. Include the grocery bill of $500, and add gas and vehicle wear-and-tear costs. Now your overall price for grocery shopping is $560 per week. As a formula, it would look like this:

Time-life value units + Food + Driving expenses = Overall price.

Here's my thinking. What if you could hire that process out for $560 *or less*? Would you then become more efficient with your time? It might allow you to set up a day trade where you make $700 or set up a swing trade that eventually pays you $1,500! Heck, it frees you up to take a nap, work out, read a book, make phone calls, or connect with your lover. It frees you up to do anything you please. Can you see how knowing your time-life value allows you to use currency to buy your time back, freeing you up for other tasks?

But here's a monkey wrench. Many individuals will feel paralyzed or be unable to pull the trigger because they'll see their money *leaving* their bank accounts and the scarcity mindset will kick in: "I can't do that! If I spend $560 to buy back three hours of time per week, then I'll have $560 less than I have now, and I won't have *gained* anything. I'll have only lost money."

This is usually a subconscious thought occurring on a micro level that you might be unable or unwilling to perceive. If you take nothing else from this book, take this:

Money is your *least* valuable asset.

Yep. You read that right. You might think I'm two chicken nuggets short of a delicious meal, but it's the truth.

Go one step further: Intangible assets are *always more valuable* than tangible ones.

Time is your most valuable asset. That's why it's at the start of the book! If you master your time, become ultra-efficient, understand how you spend and invest it, and track how you appropriate it, you will begin to master yourself. And when you master yourself, you master the markets!

I have created five wildly easy tips to help you master your time!

Tip #1: Get TSA PreCheck

"But, Jeremy, I only fly once a year!" It's still worth it. TSA PreCheck, which lasts for five years at a time, costs less than $100 and two to three hours of your time to set it up. However, it will drastically reduce your stress at airports! It decreases the amount of time you have to spend *at* the airport waiting in line. It's a must-have investment unless you literally will never step foot on an airplane. I'd happily pay ten times the going rate for TSA PreCheck simply because I value my health (less stress always equals better health), my time, my sanity, and I think taking off my shoes and walking through the metal screener in my socks is asinine.

This tip teaches your brain that your time is *very valuable!*

Tip #2: OCO Orders

While the first tip has little to do with trading, this one has everything to do with it. An OCO, or one-cancels-the-other, order is a function that allows a trader to have a stop-loss and a target set up simultaneously. If the stop-loss hits, the target gets canceled and vice versa.

Most good brokers and platforms will allow you to set up a trade, an entry to get into your position, whether it's a day trade, swing trade, futures, commodities, forex, options, or stocks. And then, once you have your entry and get filled, the broker automatically places your target and stop-loss for you.

This function allows for pretty seamless trading without having to be chained to your computer. With $100,000 of trading capital and a broker that allows OCO orders, I can make $100,000 a year working four to five hours a month. Sounds ludicrous, but such is trading. That's probably why you're reading this book. You love trading! You're addicted to it. You want to master it. Trading allows flexibility, freedom, and rewards for people who are aggressive, fearless, calculated, disciplined, and focused.

This tip assures your brain that you can release control and allow external systems to help you grow your money.

Tip #3: Get Coaching on Your Platform

Since you are vigorously working toward becoming a full-time Real Life Trader, you must use a trading platform. For 2024 and beyond, you are probably using Charles Schwab, Fidelity, TradeStation, Robinhood, or Interactive Brokers. Whichever company you use, be sure to find a professional, someone who has spent years on the platform, to show you the hard-hitting tools your platform has. Usually these brokers' walk-throughs are either free (if you get someone from the company to help you with it) or cost less than $200. You can also find loads of free tutorials on YouTube for your trading platform.

This is an extremely rewarding investment of time and money. You'll learn the platform, become better equipped, shorten your learning curve, and, ultimately, know precisely how to implement orders and make tweaks and adjustments. You'll avoid dumb mistakes and save both time and likely money. This is exactly why **Tip #2** and **Tip #3** go hand in hand.

I've learned about every broker listed above and many others, so I can give guidance, tips, and tricks for making your trading better!

Let's face it, for traders, pressing the right buttons at the right time is how you make your money. Invest in that button-pressing capability. Make sure you're extremely comfortable, fast, and flawless, and you'll perform like a professional. Your brain wants you to be a professional.

This tip allows you to feel like a professional.

Tip #4: "Time to Think" Challenge

This is going to be a tough one to swallow.

Imagine sitting with your thoughts for half a day. Nothing else—just you and your thoughts for twelve … full … hours.

I was first introduced to this mode of thinking, this radical belief system, this wild, crazy, harebrained, life-changing idea by a mentor, Andy Christiansen.

About eight years ago, we were having lunch, and he said, "When was the last time you took a day to think?"

My reply was, "I think all the time, man. I'm always thinking."

And he said, "Yeah, man, everyone does that level of thinking. The in-the-car, in-the-shower, before-you-go-to-sleep, while-you're-eating-your-lunch-alone-in-your-office kind of thinking. That's what everyone does. But you don't want to be everyone, do you? You strive for greatness, right?"

"Go on." I said.

So Andy gave me a challenge. He said, "I want you to go to a park from sunup to sundown. Take only water, a notebook, and a pen. This needs to be during the work week, so take a day off from *work* and go *think*. Go dream, plan, create, be, for twelve hours."

My friend, I was Shakespearean with that pen! The first two hours were liberating and fun! I found it easy and refreshing.

The next two hours, however, were hard. Nothing came out. No unique thoughts, nothing vibrant or saucy. Zero substance.

The next two hours, not one new idea came into my mind. I was rehashing the same old garbage, the same lame ideas, beliefs, and junk.

The next two hours, I just walked around the park. I was getting really hungry at this point. I mean, Andy said bring water. I was *fasting*, and I didn't even know it. I hadn't consumed food since dinner the previous day, and I was well into the 2:00 pm hour. I felt like I was wasting so much time! At hours eight, nine, ten, and eleven, it was nothing but negative inner talk, mental bugs, mind hurdles, too many fears to count, and thoughts of quitting.

But, the twelfth hour ... brilliant ideas came in the twelfth hour, but only after I was annoyed, frustrated, tired, and a bit hangry.

The twelfth hour was when I realized that I wasn't in the relationship I wanted to be in.

The twelfth hour was the moment I discovered how to add tremendous value to my company!

The twelfth hour was my breakthrough. And you'll experience the same, I'm certain of it.

"Everything you crave, all of your deepest desires, wants, and
needs are on the other side of fear and discomfort."
—Will Smith

I've given this twelve-hour challenge to thousands of people since I first completed it, but only around 20 percent actually accomplish it. The fear of missing out, the fear of being alone with your thoughts, the fear of spending time with no predetermined outcome creeps into the minds of most.

This "Time to Think" challenge may appear useless and anxiety-provoking and trigger thoughts like:

- "But I will miss fantastic trade setups."
- "I will miss out on money."
- "I will just be wasting my time."

The truth is the opposite. Think about Aristotle, Jesus, Buddha, Rumi, and Socrates; they were so elegantly wise and brilliant because they had loads of time to think, to be in silence, to ponder, and to create.

In silence we hear the most.

This tip helps you know, see, and understand what freedom of time actually feels like!

Tip #5: Snag YouTube Premium

YouTube is the number one place I go to learn something new. It will only continue to grow and flourish. And, right now, you can subscribe to YouTube Premium advertisement-free for $13.99 a month. Uh, yes please. I'll take two.

With YouTube Premium, you can download anything you want to watch later and minimize the application on your mobile device while doing other things. Premium is so valuable, especially if you use YouTube, which you likely do.

This tip teaches your brain that you can optimize anything in your day-to-day life.

Sweet! You are only a few pages into the book, and already you have easy and valuable tips to become more efficient!! Now that you're aware of time management and efficiencies, I'm going to show you how to even further optimize that most valuable asset!

CHAPTER 3 :
MASTER TIME OPTIMIZATION AND YOU WILL MASTER THE MARKETS

Time stress shifted for me dramatically when I began to regularly schedule events far in the future—up to three months in the future. This is how I stay on top of my game!

If I get a request from someone to take me out to breakfast to pick my brain, I either say no or I book it out at least three weeks from the time of the request. Sometimes even a month or two.

Dinner with friends? I check my upcoming calendar to see if there's an optimal near-future time to visit. Otherwise, you guessed it, I schedule it out at least three weeks, nice and far into the future.

Why three weeks? It is a very tangible and valid starting point.

I noticed (aside from work commitments) that most calendars become pretty boring and not slammed at about two weeks out. By scheduling everything out three or more weeks, I am creating my schedule so far in advance that it allows my life and activities to happen *for* me and no longer *to* me.

This includes birthdays, vacations, workout routines, 29029 Everesting training, Ironman training, writing this book, writing any book, and creating new classes and programs. I schedule them all out super far in advance, and you can too!

I'm certainly not preaching this as the only tweak you'll ever need in your life, but I can speak from experience that it works extremely well.

After I have the bulk of my events, plans, dinners, meetings, assignments, charity work, galas, trips, vacations, and speaking engagements planned out three weeks to three months in advance, I attack my day-to-day life with intention.

In one singular, *intentional* hour, I can very easily work out, shower, read three to five pages of a book, eat, make a phone call to a potential client, check emails, and hopefully even generate some income. All before 8:00 am!

Am I a weirdo about this? Sure. I am very quick, wildly intentional, ridiculously punctual, and a total time beast. I move *fast* ... 90 percent of the time.

For the other 10 percent of my time, I lounge. Hard. I schedule (yes, three months in advance) hours or sometimes days of movie marathons, pizza, naps, chess, and milkshakes. But it is planned, created, and thought through ahead of time.

Scheduling your time in advance and breaking it down into small segments will help you realize how long you actually need to accomplish most tasks. You do not need thirty minutes to take a shower. You can absolutely take that long if you really, truly want to. Spend the most time on what gives you joy, ideas, power, and purpose.

If working out for two hours straight scares you, then work out for ten minutes rather than not at all. There are thousands of ten-minute or less really shreddy style workouts on YouTube!

For those who perpetually do not have time to read a whole book, read one page a day, which takes three minutes.

You have the time; you're just wasting it. You have the time to do anything you truly prioritize!

I live my life in increments of ten minutes because I've realized that anything I need to get done, I should be able to do in that amount of time.

I think about my daily twenty-four hours in what I call time blocks. These ten-minute time blocks are sections throughout the day where I know what I should do, when, where, how often, and with what kind of speed and diligence.

Every day has 1,440 minutes (24 hours) to invest and use. Image A reflects a full day divided into 144 ten-minute blocks.

JERREMY ALEXANDER NEWSOME

IMAGE A

	:00	:10	:20	:30	:40	:50	
12							am
01							
02							
03							
04							
05							
06							
07							
08							
09							
10							
11							
12							pm
01							
02							
03							
04							
05							
06							
07							
08							
09							
10							
11							

IMAGE B

	:00	:10	:20	:30	:40	:50	
12							am
01							
02							
03							
04							
05							
06							
07							
08							
09							
10							
11							
12							pm
01							
02							
03							
04							
05							
06							
07							
08							
09							
10							
11							

In Image B, I've carved out 125 blocks to illustrate a sample day:

- two blocks for trading
- four blocks for family time
- two blocks for working out
- three blocks for eating
- four blocks for self-development
- two blocks for helping others
- eight blocks for commuting when I can listen to podcasts, audio books, and generate ideas of growth
- fifty blocks for working
- fifty blocks for sleeping

That means I'm working full time, sleeping eight hours a day, trading for twenty minutes a day, spending forty minutes with family, working out, eating, engaging in self-development, helping others, and empowering myself during my commute.

And there's still nineteen blocks left!

One of my mentors, Jesse Itzler, says, "I'm never too tired to play with my kids." He knows what it takes to make time for family, and he makes it. And that man is a certified savage!! Make sure you follow him on Instagram, and enjoy his wonderful and uplifting content.

Your children would rather spend quality time with you when you're present in the moment, playing their games with them, sitting on the floor with them and getting into their world, eating lollipops or snacking on popcorn. Children don't want to spend seven hours with you where your focus is not on them. They don't feel listened to, and they don't feel like you care. Forty minutes a day, or four blocks, might not always be possible, so try for two blocks per day where you're fully there mentally, physically, and emotionally with your kids.

And, bonus, you'll stop stressing out about how much time you *do not* spend with your kids because you'll know that you'll spend at least twenty minutes any given day.

And, per the message of this chapter, you can lock in more time with your kids in your schedule, nice and far out in the future, and then, simply make it happen! It's a win-win for all!

Regarding sleep, get as much sleep as you need. I used to believe the adages, "Sleep when you're dead" and "Sleep is for the broke." When I changed this to, "Sleep is for the wealthy; it is a remarkable way to heal and upgrade," sleep became easier for me.

I ultimately trained my body to sleep when I am tired and, when I wake up, to stay awake until I get sleepy again. When I'm tired, instead of filling my face with caffeine, I take a ten- to twenty-minute nap/rest/closed-eye meditation. *Yes*, I set alarms *just in case*, but midday naps are a favorite activity of mine.

What about eating? How do you use three ten-minute blocks to eat? Obviously, food is a must for everyone, so get creative with your food purchasing and prep.

You could hire someone to do your grocery shopping or use food delivery services. You could also invest time in meal preparation. Some of my friends do marathon cooking on Sundays so that they don't have to cook during the week. Spend twenty to thirty blocks every Sunday making food, even if it's just chicken, rice, and broccoli. Simple, easy, fast, yummy. You'll free up additional time every day during the following week, and that's how you build time wealth!

Why dedicate entire chapters to time?

Because time is your most valuable asset.

You have the time to finish this book.

You have the time to trade, invest, study, and grow.

You have the time to become a better version of yourself!

The best version of yourself absolutely slays the markets, crushes gains, attracts wins, and profits daily, weekly, and monthly!

But, if you find yourself stressed about time, that stress and pressure will affect your trading. Your subconscious mind believes, "I need to take this sub-par trade now, to hopefully make more money now, so I can escape my stress and pressure of not having any time … now."

That is a very unprofitable loop.

For a wildly profitable career and life, master time, calendars, scheduling, and optimization to step into new atmospheres of possibilities and outcomes.

CHAPTER 4 :
MASTER LOSING AND YOU WILL MASTER THE MARKETS

"You can make money every single day in the stock market.
Sometimes, it's just for someone else."
—Jerremy Alexander Newsome

I've yet to experience anything as rabidly frustrating as losing on a trade.

Why does it throw me into a mental tizzy every single time?

Because I dedicated hours of time, energy, and money and then had to *give more* of my money away.

Imagine a beautiful set up, a gorgeous hammer bouncing off long-term moving averages, great stock, a solid company, a delicious trend, and, suddenly, *doink*, it drops and stops you out, then rallies to new all-time highs days later.

WHHHHHHHHYYYYYYYYY??!?!?!?!?!

- "The market is rigged."
- "I suck at this."
- "It's the market-makers hunting stops."
- "The bid-ask spread was too wide."

The president said something stupid, some news came out, a tree fell in the woods, who cares? You lost money. You can blame it on anything you want. And it may be totally justified.

Regardless of which profession you're pursuing in life, you have to fail, lose, suck, finish last, get burned, scorched, punched, fired, cry, weep, lose it all, consider quitting everything, hit rock bottom, change your entire world, and then bounce back in order to succeed.

Read that paragraph again. It's a formula for success. Take a highlighter and mark every stage that has happened to you thus far.

Is it *the* formula?

Do you have to go through pain, heartache, and tribulation to win, succeed, and make it?

No. But you'll appreciate the wins a hell of a lot more when you have.

You will eventually lose. It's going to suck. And, honestly, no words will help. Besides, it's not going to be words that you need, it's going to be action.

You need to get comfortable with losing and altering the negative emotions attached to taking a loss on a trade. You may feel a lack of control; you may not be able to accept being wrong; you may think maybe you're not a good enough or smart enough trader; you may fear letting down your parents or your spouse. You may be quickly overcome by all of these emotions the moment you take a loss on your trade.

So how do you overcome the negative emotions attached to losing on a trade in order to get better at trading?

Lose more. The only way to get better at something is by repeating it. So here is my challenge for you.

Choose a sport or game that you're decent at; play against people who are better than you; put money on the line; and prepare to lose. Yep, I suggest you find ways to lose your money to train your emotional reactions to better serve you. You either become comfortable being uncomfortable, or you become too comfortable being comfortable. For traders, the former is always better.

In October 2021, I hosted one of my popular life-altering events called "Money Grows on Trees" at an all-inclusive resort in the Turks and Caicos, where we were surrounded by perfect beaches and idyllic water. A year prior to this conference, I had made a wager with a friend of mine named Chris. We both grew absolutely outrageous beards for an entire year, and the gamble culminated in a chess match for charity where the loser had to shave off his face trophy.

We sat down at the resort, started playing chess, and I began like most newbies—with a heart full of optimism and zero pitfalls in my way. Only opportunity and possibility lay ahead! Nevermind that I had only played chess fifteen times in my entire life up to this point.

My strategy was to take all of Chris's pieces.

Apparently, this wasn't a winning chess strategy.

I came back to Nashville clean shaven, looking like I was once again sixteen years old.

I lost like a professional (in front of everyone). But walking back to my hotel room and for the next two hours, I was fuming and humiliated! The expletives that were being thrown around in my brain toward myself would have upset Gary Vaynerchuk.

Was it because my man mane was no longer flowing in the wind when I walked?

Was it because I'd be donating a few thousand dollars to charity?

Was it because I truly suck at most board games?

Nope. I was aggravated simply because I had lost. (I would've shaved my beard off anyway because I love soup, and, if you have a two-foot-long beard, soup is a pipe dream.)

I hate losing. I'd rather slide down a balsa wood slip-n-slide naked than lose, well, *anything* really.

Where does this pain and anguish come from?

The pain of losing is derived from a scarcity mindset.

- "If I lose this money, I will have less money, and I need lots of money to survive."
- "If I lose this chess match, people will think less of me, and I'll be unable to command their attention and respect."
- "If I lose this trade, I'm not good enough or smart enough. Therefore, I'll prove my dad/mom right when they said that one time that I'll never amount to anything."

These are the dark mind ninjas that mess with you when you sleep, when you eat, when you listen to music, and when you lose on trades.

What you must do is begin to switch your brain from *losing* to *recycling*. From "I don't have enough" to "I'm circulating money." From *failing* to *gaining a loss*.

When you lose on a trade, take deep breaths into your diaphragm to calm your nervous system, which will slow down the emotions. Then, focus on how you're only upset because you lost the trade. Realize that everything is okay, it's just a trade. There's no need to panic or get scared, angry, and crazed. The only thing that matters is that you accept the loss and move on to your next trade, taking positive energy with you.

> "Fear lives in a scarcity mindset and dies in an abundant mindset."
> —Jerremy Alexander Newsome

Here are six things I do when I'm on a legitimate losing streak to clear my mind and soul and rescue my trading account:

1. Do Something I've Never Done Before

I either go somewhere new, read a new book, or play a new sport—something fresh and exciting. It clears my mind and reminds me I am capable of doing great things!

2. Volunteer

"Someone always has it worse than I do." These are important words to live by. If I'm on a losing streak, I consider my situation. I have food on the table at all times (probably too much), and I live in a nice home. There are millions of people in the world who can't say that. Therefore, I not only reflect on what I've been blessed with, but I try to contribute to others in need, and that always makes me smile.

3. Watch Motivational Videos

There are a plethora of these on YouTube. Many are very good. I probably watch at least one a week, regardless of my trading success. But, during a noticeable losing streak, I watch four to five a day.

4. Hit the Gym

Nothing breaks people out of a funk like endorphin-generating physical activity.

5. Don't Be Afraid of the Next Trade

Remember, some of the best traders in the world lose more than 50 percent of their trades. If you're 0 for 9, probability states that a win is coming. If you're a 50/50 trader (like me), and you lose five in a row, your next five could be winners. Knowing how to mitigate risk keeps the first five losses small and containable.

6. Don't Try a New Strategy

You know what works. Keep doing that. Don't reinvent the wheel. If you're a professional Real Life Trader, you'll have losing trades, losing days, and even losing weeks. But you know how to trade. Focus on what you do best, and keep doing it.

Another strategy to avoid slipping into the scarcity mindset is an abundance exercise. Try this one during your next losing trade.

Following your loss, think about how many grains of sand are on the

Earth or how many trees are on the planet. Begin counting them, and really place your thoughts and intentions on their abundance.

What you focus on can change over time. Maybe it's water droplets, atoms, leaves, ants, or pairs of sunglasses. Just think global! Ponder the vastness of time and space.

This simple exercise will subconsciously allow your brain to notice abundance; therefore, your loss will become insignificant within the bigger scheme of things, and you'll see the other side of that trade!

Perhaps the person on the other end of the computer needed the money more than you. Yours was a small contribution, a gift you can say, to the trader who outplayed you. These losses should be viewed as beautiful equilibrium moments in giving and taking from each other, the purest form of circulating money. That's what active trading is.

When you let that sink in and become comfortable with giving and receiving, having and taking, owning and selling, the emotions subside and you realize that "Rome wasn't built in a day," but it was built every day.

Ask yourself these questions, and answer honestly:

- What does it mean to you to lose on a trade?
- What meaning do you attach to losing?
- How does it make you feel?
- Do you feel incompetent, undisciplined, and unintelligent?
- Inadequate, like a failure or a loser?

What all these feelings have in common is the attachment to the result.

Experiencing negative associations when you lose on a trade doesn't mean those labels are accurate. I know it's easier to read it and think it than to believe it. When I lose, I have to rely on prior examples of when I lost to easily make back everything and then some, reaffirming my mindset. Learn to embrace the losses and the mistakes. There's a huge difference between losing and failing.

Everyone loses in life. You can lose your car keys. You can lose a game of chess, monopoly, or basketball.

But failing is giving up with no tangible reward.

Failing is experiencing pain, loss, and hardship and not allowing yourself to create memories, magic, and lessons.

Failing is being unable to see the positive that was there in each part of life. Each event either happened to you or for you.

The most profound shift I ever made in my trading career relates to losing. When I lose on a trade, I imagine a person, a friend on the other side of the world, taking my money. I'm giving my money *to them*, honoring them with my gift. It always feels good to give to others. Like the Love Doctor, Anil Gupta, says, "If you want to live more, you must give more."

This circulation of generosity directly places you in a state of giving and of gratitude, which replaces your mindset of fear and scarcity with abundance and overflow.

When you lose, your mind has been trained to go to scarcity because you're scared. You're scared of losing your money, losing your security, losing the love, support, and trust of your family, losing it all. It's an avalanche of emotions.

So you have to rewire those neural pathways; reprogram your mind to focus on the vastness of what is available to you.

I understand that losing is frustrating and that you don't like it. Trust me, I've been there. But by practicing shifting from a scarcity mindset to an abundance mindset on every loss, you train yourself to see losing as part of the game and not the end of it.

What helps hundreds of thousands of traders master losing is truly understanding risk. In the Foreword (you read the Foreword, right?), Dennis mentions my concept of risk and how I teach it and present it (the R system). The more you become fully aware of the certainty this provides, the more you can approach the markets in a controlled manner.

CHAPTER 5 :
MASTER RISK AND YOU WILL MASTER THE MARKETS

Thousands of traders have shared with me their woes about winning small, winning small, winning small, and then, poof, one giant loss wipes out all of the gains.

Has this happened to you?

I'm sure it has.

The solution to this problem is keeping your risk the same on every single trade over a long period of time.

If you are an avid follower of my work, and thank you for that by the way, you are very familiar with the R system.

But for those who need a more beefy description of how to master risk, let's dive in!

The "r" in the R system stands for risk unit.

And what is a risk unit? It's a way of thinking about trades that takes the emphasis off of risking *money*. It is no longer money that you trade, it's just risk units. Boring, plain old risk units. By labeling it differently, you break the visceral connection to the notion of risking money by trading risk instead.

The R system creates certainty in your trades. Humans crave certainty; it is a basic human need from a psychology standpoint. With more certainty in your life, you will feel more safe and protected, which further breaks the emotional bond with money that is crucial for rapidly accelerating your finances.

Your goal with the R system is risk small, win big. Cut your losers and let your winners run. Risk less than your potential reward. You know, all of that terminology. Here is how you should calculate it.

The R you trade should be approximately 2% of your entire account. It can certainly be less. It can be 1% or 0.5% even or 0.25%. *You* determine your risk percentage. Usually, and especially for newer traders, the smaller the better when starting out.

For example: You have a $5,000 account. You select your R as 2%. $5,000 x .02 = $100. In this example, your risk is $100.

Note: I am **not** saying that you can only spend $100 per trade.

I'm simply stating that $100 is the amount you would be *willing to lose* on trades.

That's your risk unit, or your R. The amount of investment, or your position size, is not the focus here. In my opinion, the more important factor is the potential risk on each trade, i.e., how much you'll lose if you're wrong.

Like Warren Buffett said, "The first rule of an investment is don't lose [money]. The second rule of an investment is don't forget the first rule. And that's all the rules there are."

Your goal with trading is to *lose as little money as possible*. Risk mitigation and defense should be your concern and focus. If you prevent yourself from completely destroying your account, you can trade for longer. After all, trading does require money!

How to Calculate Your R With Shares

R / stop value = amount of shares to trade

A trader wants to enter AAPL (Apple Inc.), and she plans to buy shares as it bounces off $120 as a support price. She looks at the chart and determines $118 to be a good price for a stop. The stop value in this scenario is $2, which is the difference between the entry price and the stop location.

Let's say she has an R of $100.

R = $100 / $2 stop value = 50 shares to trade. Her investment would be $120 x 50 shares, or $6,000. Her risk, however, if she is wrong is only a $100 loss.

Let's look at the same trader but a different stock.

She wants to enter META (Meta Platforms, Inc., previously Facebook, Inc.), and she plans to buy shares as it bounces off $81 as a support price. She looks at the chart and determines $80 to be a good price for a stop. The stop value in this scenario is $1.

R = $100 / $1 stop value = 100 shares to trade. Her investment would be $81 x 100 shares, or $8,100. Her risk, however, if she's wrong is only a $100 loss.

Two different stocks, same loss potential. Therefore, if META goes up and AAPL stops out for a loss, she can be right only 50 percent of the time and still make a profit. If META bounces from $81 and goes up to $90 and makes 9R on this trade, while only 1R is lost on the AAPL trade, she's gained a total of 8R, or $800. This trader created a plan, followed it, mitigated losses, and made a profit. Boom. That is what it looks like to be a Real Life Trader!

CHAPTER 6 :
MASTER YOUR TRADING PLAN AND YOU WILL MASTER THE MARKETS

A trading plan should have rules that prevent you from losing money.

And the only way to know if you can follow those rules is by following them for a solid period of time, like three months.

A day trading plan would look something like this.

1. Only move my stop once I've been in the trade for twenty minutes.
2. I can only day trade between 10:00 am and 1:00 pm New York time.
3. I have to write down my plan on the asset on the chart at least five minutes before I get into the position.
4. I can only take a maximum of four day trades per day.
5. My maximum loss per day is 2R.
6. My maximum loss per week is 5R.
7. I will only day trade TSLA, NVDA, COIN, SQ.
8. I will exit all day trades at 1.2R until I have 6R of realized profits locked in.

These are good rules for new day traders to adopt.

In Chapter 5, I introduced you to the R system. In this chapter, I will blend how to master risk and your trading plan so you can master the markets.

Let's get to it.

You have a $50,000 account, and you chose to have a 1% R. That's $500 of risk.

Could you have a $500R for the first three to four months of your day trading as you learn this skill and craft? Absolutely!

And, ultimately, after two years of trading and an account that has doubled to $100,000, you could double your risk units to $1,000R.

A $1,000R can be life changing, especially for those with good discipline.

Look at our trader from Chapter 5. Change her R in the two trading scenarios (Apple and Meta) to $1000.

For AAPL, R = $1000 / $2 stop value = 500 shares to trade. Her investment would be $120 x 500 shares, or $60,000.

For META, R = $1000 / $1 stop value = 1000 shares to trade. Her investment would be $81 x 1000 shares, or $81,000.

If META bounces from $81 and goes up to $90 and makes 9R on this trade, while only 1R is lost on the AAPL trade, she's gained a total of 8R, or $8000!

Imagine 8R a month, or $8,000 a month, in addition to your

current income. Sounds pretty damn good. Pay down debts, begin to buy assets, improve your home, take trips. Do whatever you want to do.

Just know that the process probably takes longer than you expect, and definitely takes longer than you want (because it's just human nature to want everything to happen immediately, always).

What would a basic trading plan look like for someone who is swing trading?

1. Only move my stop once I've been in the trade for eight days.
2. I can only place my swing trade when the market is closed.
3. I can't adjust my swing trade while the market is open.
4. I have to write down my plan on the asset on the chart at least twelve hours before I get into the position.
5. I can only be in six swing trades at once.
6. I must only trade with the trend.
7. I will have analyzed the daily, weekly, and monthly charts before placing a trade.
8. I will use the 78-minute chart and daily chart as my primary time frames to enter my swing trade.
9. If I am profitable on all of my swing trades simultaneously, I will exit them all to lock in gains.

Trading plans are wildly useful and horrifically underutilized by most active traders.

I hand out basic trading plans like candy canes during Christmas at www.reallifetrading.com. Pop over there, log into the dashboard, click on the icons, and snag yourself some totally free trading plans!

CHAPTER 7 :
MASTER YOUR MONEY AND
YOU WILL MASTER THE MARKETS

"Today be thankful and think how rich you are. Your family is priceless,
your time is gold and your health is wealth."
—Zig Ziglar

You can have a relationship with money.

And you can make that relationship better.

The intention of this chapter is to help you improve your relationship with currency and money.

Everyone I've ever met wants more money. Why? Because money creates freedom. And everyone craves the freedom to have more experiences, more travel, more moments, and more magic! And money provides these.

Trading the markets to make money is like swimming in the ocean. You will need to be very comfortable with the tides, the waves, and the current of currency.

How do you get more comfortable with money?

Think of your best friend. In your mind, say their name. Describe your relationship.

What are you saying?

What words are you using?

Maybe it sounds something like this:

Svetlana, you're such a vibrant and caring person. I'm a better person for knowing you. I improve each day and week because you're in my life. You help me and allow me to pour my light into the world.

I'll stop here for brevity's sake. I could write to my wife, Svetlana, for days.

Now change your best friend's name to Money, and repeat the above statement.

Money, you're so vibrant and caring. I'm a better person for knowing you. I improve each day and week because you're in my life. You help me and allow me to pour my light into the world.

This is how you improve your relationship with money. Treat *it* like someone you care about. Money has very similar vibrational frequencies to music. The difference is that you hear music, but you feel money. If you want more music in your life, you know exactly how to get it. You crank up the volume knob. If you want more money in your life, crank up the feeling knob.

If you're looking to trade full time, I must ask why.

Is it for the money it can bring you? Trading can undoubtedly bring in lots of money. And you want to be rich! Fantastic. Everybody does.

But, if you're attracted to trading simply because you can make money doing it, know that there are much more *guaranteed* ways to create income and cash flow.

To succeed at and enjoy trading, you must be excited about the nuances of trading—the mechanics, the charts, and the mental complexities. You must crave the challenges, those mind grenades, that it represents—the uncapped opportunities, the daily variety, the change that becomes cemented into the charts for history after price action unfolds, the battle between buyers and sellers, between the fearful and the optimistic. You must expect to be in a love-hate relationship for four to five years! The stakes are high, the thrills even higher.

Active trading is not passive income. This profession is definitely not for someone looking to coast and take it easy. But, done correctly, you can elevate your money, time, and magic!

If you want the freedom of time, then you're going to want to *trade less*, my friend. All things being equal, which would you choose: trading twelve hours a month to make $5,000 or trading a hundred hours a month to make $5,000? The obvious answer is actually attainable … by letting the energy flow and keeping it simple. Come up with a strategy, system, and approach to trade less and make more.

Consider the equation $600 x 200 = $120,000.

That equation represents a $600 net gain per day for 200 days of active trading. You can achieve this by trading only TSLA for two hours a day, four days a week for 200 days in a given year. "What?! Trade only one stock?!" Yes! It's doable! "But I thought you had to trade a basket of stocks to make money?" Nope. The money is there in the market; and the market gives it to those who walk the path of self-discipline.

Self-discipline is careful thought about all of the relationships in your life and taking proper action to improve them. Money is one of those relationships, but, in the next chapter, I'll shed light on a relationship that's even more important for blissful happiness!

CHAPTER 8 :
MASTER YOUR FAMILY AND
YOU WILL MASTER THE MARKETS

This is a direct message I received from someone in my Real Life Trading organization.

This day trader had a losing streak running for about four months. He was doing everything in his power to make money from trading, but he just couldn't turn a profit at the end of the month.

I suggested he not be so hard on himself. He was spending fourteen hours a day grinding over charts and placing trades, unable to spend time with his wife and his family.

He was battling many of the stresses, pressures, and challenges I've written about thus far: time, money, losing, and, now, family pressures.

Hey Jerremy, I know it is probably frustrating to have me messaging you all the time and I know it seems super stupid to fret over five shares. I have not really made much trading, so if these five shares move in the wrong direction, it will basically put me in the red for the month. My ability to succeed has just become so much more important. I have one good day, followed by multiple red days. Then I see all sorts of posts, from so many people, about how easy it is to make money right now. Are other people not having all these red days? I just do not get it, am I missing an edge, am I lacking a strategy? I am just going crazy trying to figure it out and I am overwhelmed in what to do outside of trading to make money. I really wish I could say I have doubled my accounts in February, and I had bought March, but I have not. My wife is finally starting to grow less and less supportive, as I have shown no profits for almost four months. I guess I can understand her concerns, we have a family. If I cannot make money trading, then I really should not be spending time doing it. I feel like I should be able to have a month without a red day, yet I just cannot seem to do it. How are so many people able to find success within six months, are they lying? I have been working on my mindset, that is not really helping either. My mindset cannot determine whether the trade works or not, and whether the setup is good or not. I am trying everyday, man, and I am at my wit's end and fresh out of time to see if trading is going to work for me. I need this to work, or I need to pull the plug, again I know this is not your problem.

I'm sure you can feel his frustration, anger, animosity, stress, all the things.

There is so much embedded in this post. It's a reflection of the many real-life challenges traders face and my biggest reason for writing this book!

Let's dissect a couple sections of the message, and I'll share how I and all the profitable traders I know (including, eventually, this very client) have overcome such hurdles.

"If I cannot make money trading, then I really should not be spending time doing it. I feel like I should be able to have a month without a red day, yet I just cannot seem to do it."

Where in Newton's apple tree does he get that idea from? Going an entire month without one single red day has never happened to me in my entire trading life because there are multiple definitions of a "red day."

For example, let's say I get into a position, it goes up 10% in eight days, and, on the ninth day, it drops 2%. Am I down 2%? No. I'm down 2% *that day*, but I'm still up 8% *overall*. Technically, that ninth day could count as a red day, at least on that position and trade, but not in the bigger picture.

It's possible that by not looking at my account I could have had a day without red. Which brings me to the philosophical question: "If a tree falls in the forest with no one around to hear it, does it make a sound?" Or in trader terms; "If I don't look at my account, did I have a red day?"

Simply put, this notion of "not having a red day in any given month" is a standard I'd rather not spend any time, energy, or concern trying to achieve. Losing on a trade is easy. It's what you do after losses that defines you. Avoid trading when you're stressed out. You'll force trades, and that energy will work against you every time. It's physics 101: You push forward, the energy pushes back. (Newton's Third Law!)

Trading should be simple and kind of unexciting. If your hands sweat, your shirt is soaked, and your breathing is super shallow, there's a good chance you are risking too much or you are vastly undereducated and underprepared. Allow yourself to fall in love with the process and the market will reward you.

"The markets reward the specialist."
—Anne-Marie Baiynd

Secondly, my man above didn't have a *trading* problem per se; he had an *income* problem. What do I mean by an income problem?

"My wife is finally starting to grow less and less supportive, as I have shown no profits for almost four months. I guess I can understand her concerns, we have a family."

This trader, like many traders, has put tons of undue pressure on himself. He's trying to generate a legitimate income and living from a career in which he is not yet a professional.

Consider: If you and I played tennis every day for two years, would you expect to be able to play tennis professionally then as a means to provide for your family?

How long would you need to play tennis before you could realistically make a living off of it? Many traders go too deep, too quickly while relying on only one stream of income. And until you have at least four years of experience, you can barely call it a "stream" of income.

This lack of income is causing massive stress on his family, his wife, and their relationship. This is common for traders.

It's very possible trading will cause an intense strain on your financial situation and, thus, your relationships. But only if you allow it to. As a trader, you're directly responsible for setting realistic goals and expectations.

And, as importantly, communicate that your success is going to take longer than expected. Remember, go in with the expectation that this is your job, your career, and what you'll be doing from X time to Y time on specific days. Create a schedule, plan it far in advance (see Chapter 3!), and stick to it.

Advise your family that you don't know how much you're going to make, but you're learning as if you're going to college to become an architect. It may take years of study, but it will be worth it.

Successful relationships are built through honest and deliberate conversations. Always set expectations and openly communicate your goals and outcomes. Give positive feedback to the important people in your life. When you make some winning trades and bring in positive Rs, share the wealth with your spouse/partner! Reward them with a trip! Buy something they like! It could be a steak dinner, a new purse, a new car, a third honeymoon, it really doesn't matter. It's about doing something extravagant for them. Make the money real especially after they have supported you.

Don't forget that your children are also part of that support group. I know a trader who bought her daughter's braces after a month of strong trading. That's $7000 worth of self-improvement. This "leadher," this "she-EO," this "warriher," this "Shero" taught her daughter that wealth, generosity, and independence can come from trading the stock market. Her daughter will now have positive associations with day trading. I love these kinds of stories!

To achieve your freedom, set specific expectations and specific timelines, and inform your significant others how long this will take. Be honest and clear. It took me eight long years to make a million dollars.

As an active market participant, you want to make a living—hell, a good living—in this profession. And you probably crave doing this full time as your career.

The good news is that most people who are attempting to be professional (insert anything here: traders, athletes, chefs, business owners, house flippers) will quit or run out of money in two to three years. My ceiling can be your floor. My failures and mistakes can be where you begin. You never have to lose all your money and only eat the free samples at Costco.

Why is this good news? Because now you know your target and your finish line. Make it past that three-year mark. Know your risk, know your timeline, play small ball for a while, learn the buttons, and understand the process. Becoming a full-time Real Life Trader is one of the coolest professions anyone can have!

CHAPTER 9 :
MASTER YOUR INCOME AND
YOU WILL MASTER THE MARKETS

"Anyone who says money can't buy happiness hasn't been poor enough. I'm not talking going from six figures to seven. I'm talking from EBT to BTC."
—Ed Latimore

Why do I talk about income?

And how does income differ from money?

Income is how you stabilize your family's finances and provide everyone with certainty and security.

In Chapter 8, you read the story of a man who was struggling with trading; his life all around kind of sucked.

But, it would suck *a lot* less if he continued bringing in income and still found ways to trade. Continuous and reliable income would provide him and his family with a stronger foundation from which he could build a profitable trading career.

More cash flow streams = less stress = more money = more happiness = better trading = more cash flow streams = less stress.

It's a spectacular cycle! If you quit your job to only have one stream of income—in this case, trading—then you are no better off than you were at work with one income stream.

I believe that:

- The *safest* way to build cash flow is real estate.
- The *fastest* way to create cash flow is liquid market trading.
- The *easiest* way to create cash flow is sales.

Real estate, while the safest investment for building cash flow (due to its tax advantages and potential for passive income), is also the slowest and most cumbersome. It demands a lot of research, a lot of cash up front, and a lot of patience for eventual appreciation.

Trading, on the other hand, is a very fast way to create cash flow. The term "liquid market trading" comes from the enormous liquidity that the markets offer. On any given day, hundreds of billions of U.S. dollars move in and out of the U.S. stock market.

If you want to trade in the liquid markets, stocks, cryptocurrencies, futures, forex, commodities, bonds, etc., there are no phone calls you need to make. No customers, invoices, refunds, repairs, returns, updates, tweaks, emails, tenants, contracts, traffic jams, or boring breakfast meetings. It's you and a laptop.

If you need to go in and make $20,000,000 in a day, a week, a month, or a lifetime, you can. The market will neither care nor notice. Twenty million to the market isn't even a grain of sand on the leg of a fly that's buzzing above the ocean compared to what moves in and out of the markets on a daily basis.

So if trading is the fastest way to create cash flow, what's the easiest?

Sales.

"But I don't have anything to sell," you might say.

The truth is, we are all in sales, all the time, every day. You're selling yourself on what to eat, which clothes to wear, what music to listen to, which coffee cup to use, and so forth. Being able to determine if someone else will truly benefit from a product is a remarkable skill. When you approach sales from the standpoint of service and alignment, money will begin flowing to you.

Understanding sales, the complexities of it, studying it, embracing it, and interacting with it will always be the easiest way to become a multimillionaire.

"If it's so easy, Jerremy, then why doesn't everyone do it?" Because it's easier not to.

That's the answer I give on most attributes of success. It's all easy. Becoming rich is simple.

> "You will get all you want in life if you help enough
> other people get what they want."
> —Zig Ziglar

And that's the premise of sales. I have a program called "Sales Samurai" where I provide eight weeks of real-world examples to transform an individual's sales experience and comfort level.

I wanted to put this chapter into a trading psychology book because it's okay for you as a full-time trader to have multiple streams of income.

Heck, it's encouraged! Extra income will get you through those rough market months, which will happen to every single trader reading this book. Remember, money is easy, and it's everywhere. It wants to have a relationship with you and hang out with you! Stop pushing it away!

I'll use the example of me being employed at a full-time job while simultaneously trading as a second income.

If I had a losing day in that situation, I'd work even harder in my job to produce more income for the company. Perhaps I'm in the sales role and can directly increase cash flow. Or I'm in the supply chain department where I can determine a new route for prolific cost savings. Maybe I'm in management, and I can tweak an employee's mindset, improve their mood, and assist them in performing their best that day or week, which will ultimately optimize the company.

Tweaks are available everywhere, my friend. I didn't lose money, I gained a loss. I gained an opportunity to become better at something else.

If your income goal is to make $230,000 in a year, perhaps $30,000 of that is through trading. Your current job provides $120,000 of that. Now you only need $80,000 to make nearly a quarter of a million in a year.

A question you could ask often as a full-time trader is: "What product do I love, use, and believe in that would help my friends and those around me?"

Imagine that product is a bag of coffee that your friend cultivated. It's a new company and a new brand, and she would love promotion. I would ask that friend, "What's your bottom-line cost for the bag?" She says, "$7.50."

I'd buy the bags from her at $10 and attempt to sell them at $20, giving me $10 per bag of profit with zero additional costs. Now how many bags do I need to sell to make $80,000 a year? Eight thousand!

That's a lot of bags of coffee.

Well there are a lot of people in the world. Eight thousand initially sounds daunting, but divided by twelve months and then divided by four weeks, it becomes 166 to sell per week. That's more reasonable.

At this stage, I think, create, scheme, and put a plan into action. I need to go where the people are!

And, of course, as the old saying goes, "The more time you put into thinking, the less time you have to put into doing." Perhaps at this stage, I think of a person who's very influential, who happens to be my friend and has a big following on Instagram or X. I offer to pay that person $1 per bag to promote this fledgling coffee company. Now I only receive $9 of profit, but I have to do less work.

It comes down to having clarity and coming up with a process for your clarity. This is how money is created and generated, through ideas that have deadlines and meaningful goals.

When I have a losing day or week, my first reaction is to review my bad trade(s), determine what changes and alterations I can make heading into the next day, and then ponder how I can generate income for my family through other means, which is generally sales.

Here is my acronym for SALES:

Spiritually
Aligned
Language in
Everyday
Service

When you have the ability to sell your or someone else's course, product, information, book, program, or service to a person who will greatly benefit from it, that in itself is its own reward.

But there's a bonus!

Sales also relate directly to stock trading in two ways.

#1: When you understand sales are crucial in trading, it allows you to sell higher and buy lower.

#2: You'll always have a kick-ass income.

Here's how sales will help you in trading: sell high, buy low.

Usually you hear this phrase as "buy low, sell high."

Why did I say it in reverse?

When you practice sales, you'll become familiar with price battles. Buyers always want to buy for less, sellers always want to sell for higher. Always.

How does knowing this help you in trading?

It will ultimately allow you to set your limit sells even higher and place your limit buys even lower. A lot of traders buy *very* high hoping it will go higher. The stock market is the only place I've noticed that, when the price of something drops drastically, people truly become terrified of buying the same asset at lower prices.

My advice is to always try and get the best price possible. What will you do as someone who is trained in sales? Throw in a nice low bid, just in case …

If you do not *love* sales as much as I do, that is perfectly okay.

Just think about who you can connect with, network with, offer value to, write for, account for, or clean for in order to bring in additional income on top of your trading! Remember, *money grows on trees*!

CHAPTER 10 :
MASTER SCARCITY AND
YOU WILL MASTER THE MARKETS

One of my coaching students had saved $60,000 to take his family of seven on a first-class cruise through the Mediterranean Sea along Italy's coastline. I asked him when he and his family had gone on a cruise, to which he replied, "Never. I've been saving up for this one! The best of the best for my family."

His answer stunned me for a moment. I pondered his situation. He was going to spend $60,000 on a cruise not knowing if anyone in his family even liked cruises? What if someone got seasick?

Why is this a story about the scarcity mindset? My man was saving up for *years* to give his family an unforgettable experience. Isn't that abundance?

No. My coaching student was, in fact, battling a scarcity mindset about going on a smaller, less expensive cruise. He was thinking in fear that spending $5,000 on a smaller cruise to see if everyone liked the experience and had a blast would mean that he would have less money and set him back from his original goal of $60,000. His perspective was that he would have $5,000 less than he should've had.

This, my friends, was his mind being fearful of the unknown, afraid of the "what if" ... the "What if I never get my $5,000 back?"

Delaying experiences and waiting to do the things you want to do simply because buying them would plunder your assets and decrease your savings is a scarcity mindset.

A swing in perspective to an abundance mindset would be scheduling a less extravagant, less expensive weekend cruise first just to make sure everyone enjoys the cruise experience. Does it take money away from the $60,000? Technically, yes. However, it gives the family what they are looking for, and it gives my man's brain the joy, thrill, and excitement of an exotic holiday. It becomes a gain: "Let me spend $5,000, and if we create amazing, fun core memories, then it will be really easy for me to make, create, save, and invest another $5,000 next year to get me back to $60,000 needed for the bigger cruise."

Dr. Andrew Huberman has mentioned a *few* times on his podcast that "the brain is designed to seek out pleasure," so once my client experiences the pleasure of the above-mentioned cruise, his brain will find ways to feel that again. The subconscious seeks out more opportunities to increase the experience; it happens while sleeping, working, and even exercising.

"It's not death a man should fear, but he should fear never beginning to live."
—Marcus Aurelius

How is a scarcity mindset triggered?

Often by asking this as a first question:

How much will it cost?

Is it important to know the cost? Yes. Should it be your first concern? No. If it were free, would you do it? If the answer is yes, then it's a money issue holding you back. I am not saying that budgeting isn't important; knowing the monetary value of an experience is crucial. However, you should stop making that your first question.

Other initial questions should be:

- Who's attending?
- What will I learn from this experience?
- Will this be something I remember and talk about five years from now?
- Will this increase my stress level or make my life better?
- What lifelong memories will this create?

Depending on the answers to these questions, put it in the calendar! Step into abundance and prosperity! You *can* afford it. You likely have the money, you just don't see how you could both enjoy the experience and make that money back quickly.

How many of you know someone who has saved and saved their entire life, and, suddenly, they're seventy-five years old, reflecting back on their life, wondering what they have done or, more importantly, what they have *not* done?

Rather than be the person afraid to spend money because it means you'll have less money, be the person who is afraid of not living. Grab some friends or your family, and go rent a catamaran and sail around Greece for a week!

Visit my website www.treesaremoney.com, and find out what adventure I've planned to elevate wealth consciousness with some of the best humans on earth.

Some of my favorite books that challenge the scarcity mindset include *You Are a Badass*, by Jen Sincero, *A Return to Love*, by Marianne Williamson, *Awaken the Giant Within*, by Tony Robbins, *The Monk Who Sold His Ferrari*, by Robin Sharma, and *$100M Offers*, by Alex Hormozi. And there's my own book on the subject, *Money Grows on Trees*, that also guides you toward a mindset of abundance.

If you're serious about breaking the scarcity that lives in your mind and want to hear how to do it from other people just like you, try reading these books.

What are the next steps?

CHAPTER 11 :
MASTER GOAL SETTING AND
YOU WILL MASTER THE MARKETS

Most goals, dreams, and hopes can be purchased with more money.

Since you love trading … since it keeps you up at night … since the thought of huge massive candles gets you all giddy … then use it to help fuel and fulfill your dreams and goals!

Let's say you're my client from Chapter 10 who wants to go on the Mediterranean cruise. How would you begin to *master your goal setting* so this would come into your life?

You would begin by trading cruise line stocks like CCL (Carnival Cruise Lines) and NCLH (Norwegian Cruise Line Holdings)! They're priced low enough for just about anyone to be able to buy and sell 1,000 shares frequently. Pick a quick and easy momentum strategy (I'll provide one later in the book in case you aren't already super familiar).

The goal?

Make $12 per share with your 1,000 shares over the next one to two months.

Obtain some profits, pull them out, and pay for the cruise $400 to $500 at a time. This makes it much easier to take the profit when it's there.

Do you want to take that goal setting one step further?

Share your plan with your spouse and kids; let everyone know you're trading cruise line stocks to pay for the family cruise. Imagine the excitement when they're sharing with their friends that they're going on a cruise that you paid for by trading the stock market! This will create a positive association, and your children will remember both the cruise and the stock market forever.

Are you ready for another goal?

How about flying in first class on your next flight?

To fly in first class from Nashville to Las Vegas costs around $1,500 on Delta Air Lines.

Pull up the chart of Delta Air Lines; look for opportunities to either go long or short; and with a few hundred shares, you will begin chipping away at the costs of that first-class ticket!

CHAPTER 12 :
MASTER FEAR AND
YOU WILL MASTER THE MARKETS

A gentleman named Mark once asked me, "How do you take the leap to do something big, scary, and radical when you have a family to support?"

My answer?

"Embark on something that scares you but does not negatively impact your family."

A trader named Jon reached out to me years ago and shared the following:

> *Hey, so I just wanted to let you know that something changed in me last night after participating in your class. It did not happen immediately, although it hit me while I was sleeping. I literally jumped out of bed and started writing for hours. Let me share with you some of what I wrote.*
>
> *After a disagreement a while back with my wife, I realized I never supported her choices regarding the family's future as well as her*

career. I finally got the nerve to have a large conversation with her, where I asked her what she wanted in life regarding her goals. Long story short again, we both realized we needed to help the younger generation get into the skilled trades with a career path. We realized we had strong passionate feelings about this and being licensed tradespeople, we can now make a difference by creating opportunities for the younger generation.

So I eventually spent over two hours crafting notes and over five pages of ideas on how me and my wife can better and more effectively serve the younger generations of today.

First: "something changed in me last night." Jon had a breakthrough just by attending one of my classes. How exceptional is that?!

This is how true life change begins—by spending time with like-minded people, generating thoughts and ideas, and gaining new insight and perspectives you never even thought of. It's the micro-moments that will change your life if you take the time to find them, listen to them, and apply what they're teaching you. The key is the application. Take action!

Second, how impressive is it that after one of our classes together, Jon's eyes opened to a world of opportunity for him and his wife that will empower the younger generations? This is exactly why I do what I do; it inspires me to hear these stories.

Do you want to know what will be most exciting for Jon on his journey? All the new thoughts, ideas, mind maps, and mental valleys that he has never visited before. He's going to create new beliefs that will help their new lives unfold and reshape their future together. This is the power of community!

I believe breakthroughs like Jon's can happen for you ... once you master fear.

Fear is what stops you from having these revelations, these a-ha moments. It's what keeps you from obtaining the success you desire.

It's fear of the unknown that leaves you feeling uneasy and often paralyzes you. Let's go back hundreds or even thousands of years. Early humans had to be wary of the unknown because it could kill them. That tasty-looking berry that you've never seen before? Fatal. That friendly-looking animal that you've never seen before? Deadly. There was a purpose to fearing the unknown; it quite literally kept humans alive.

Fear is embedded in your DNA, and, while you are no longer running away from mountain lions, the rules about the world and the habits you learned from your ancestors have been passed down from generation to generation according to the fear that kept them alive. As a result, you don't know what you don't know, and you fear it.

The following quote from Marianne Williamson has arguably changed my life more than anything else I've ever read. (Life hack: Read this passage to your loved ones, including your kids, as often as you can! It will change your life.)

Our deepest fear is not that we are inadequate. Our deepest fear is that we are powerful beyond measure. It is our light, not our darkness, that most frightens us. We ask ourselves, who am I to be brilliant, gorgeous, talented, and fabulous? Actually, who are you not to be? You are a child of God. Your playing small does not serve the world. There is nothing enlightened about shrinking so that other people will not feel insecure around you. We are all meant to shine, as children do. We were born to make manifest the glory of God that is within us. It is not just in some of us, it is in everyone. And as we let our own light shine, we unconsciously give other people permission to do the same. As we are liberated from our own fear, our presence automatically liberates others.

According to Williamson, the fear of failing is not what holds you back. It's the fear of living and receiving your dreams while not knowing how to manage your achievements. It's a fear of success. If you have been striving your whole life to reach a certain measure of success, what will you do when you get there? Who will you be without all the striving? And once you have success, how do you keep it? That's your deepest fear, and, consequently, that's my deepest fear.

You might also have a fear of change. To be successful in your family, wealth, finances, and spirituality could disrupt your current lifestyle, and this change could alienate you from what you know and what feels comfortable.

In the deep trenches of your brain, in the synapses that were formed when you were four to forty-eight months old, a fear developed—a subconscious fear that prevents you from shining your light from Tokyo to Topeka, my friend! This fear forces you to believe that you are invalidating those around you when you shine your light, which is the opposite of your intentions. And the ones most affected by your lack of light are the people that you care about: friends, family, partners, spouses, children. In what way you might ask?

The answer is one of my favorite lines from Williamson's passage:

"Your playing small does not serve the world."

My wife told me this on March 13, 2020. She said, "Why are you playing so small? You're a king! You're a love warrior! You're holding yourself back unintentionally, and it's time for you to unleash your greatness to the world!"

What a woman.

That's why you're now reading this book. Years ago, I had beliefs like "I'm not smart enough. I'm not a great writer. I can't create proper sentence structure. I ramble when I write." And so on. But I'm no longer afraid of anyone seeing, hearing, or reading my thoughts.

> "Our words create the world we live in."
> —Britnie Turner

Small shifts regarding the words you use about yourself will create an extraordinary impact on your thoughts, your beliefs, your identity, and your future.

Remember, you're not helping anyone by avoiding pleasure, happiness, and money. And you're in no position to serve the world if you've hit rock bottom, if you're poor and broke, both mentally and financially.

Have you noticed in the podcasts you listen to, the books you read, the videos you watch on YouTube that everyone who's had one can recall, with scary precision, their rock-bottom experience?

I sure do. I even remember my rock type. It was cracked, gray concrete, the kind you find in semi-rundown neighborhoods right next to the abandoned basketball hoop.

Rock bottom is depression and anxiety. Rock bottom is poverty.

Rock bottom is the pain, anguish, and hardships that are very familiar for billions of humans on this planet.

What is unfamiliar, however, is bliss, financial nirvana, unlimited money, ample resources, loads of time, zero stress, and the ability to buy anything you want, anytime, from anywhere in the world.

The unfamiliarity of knowing with extreme precision where you'd go, how you'd get there, and what you could truly become creates fear.

It is that fear which holds so many people back because they have not tasted or experienced what's on the other side.

Do not let *fear* keep you from engaging in the very act that can change your life.

So how do you *master fear so that you will master the markets?*

Try new things! Experience realities different from your current one.

I've worked with thousands of individuals who say, "I don't have enough money to live the life that I want." But, they confess, "When I have the money in the future, I'll reward myself."

Seems like a fair statement on the surface. But my follow-up question for that person (or you) is: "How long will you deny yourself pleasure? How much longer is it going to be before you have all the money in the world to do whatever you want to do? How many months or years will it be that you prolong travel, bliss, peace, and happiness?"

In other words, "How much longer are you going to prolong life's pleasures because you're too cheap?"

Literally. If you were up for sale, you would not cost a lot. If you were a physical item, you would be on the bottom shelf, covered in dust with a giant yellow discount sticker. By saying that you'll reward yourself in the future when you have money, you are telling everyone around you along with the universe that you know your worth and your value, and that it's minuscule.

A more positive way to convey a similar message is to say, "I'm financially conscious, and I don't feel like buying a first-class plane ticket all the time, although, when the opportunity arises, I'll do it rather than just giving a series of lame excuses."

So this is my challenge to you!

Come up with five experiences you haven't yet embarked on. Be creative! Send them to me on X @newsomenuggets.

Then put those five experiences on your calendar. They can be years from now, and that's okay.

Include the dates when you'll buy the tickets, sign the deposit, or get committed. Tiny bricks build large walls.

That is how you conquer fear! Do it now, do it small, but do it!

CHAPTER 13 :
MASTER YOUR MIND AND
YOU WILL MASTER THE MARKETS

For this chapter, I want to start with a mental exercise that I learned on a Bob Proctor video. This exercise will show you why you think the way you do.

Think of your mind.

Picture an *image* of what your mind is and how it functions.

What image did you create?

Literally and figuratively, what came to mind?

The most popular answers are a machine, a factory, a light bulb, a brain.

Less popular answers are a book, an airplane, a movie, a city.

Your mind is one of your most valuable assets. How often do you change it, mold it, shape it, scare it, update it, and challenge it?

You have probably heard the term "mindset" a million times. "Mindset" is defined as "a fixed mental attitude or disposition that predetermines a person's responses to and interpretations of situations." It means your mind is set on a certain system, protocol, or belief.

When my wife and I were dating, she wanted to make sure I was ready for her "too muchness" (as she calls it). Her own journey has been one of healing her soul and cleansing her mind of toxic waste that humans naturally accumulate through stress, traumatic experiences, and/or dis-ease in the body.

So she took me to a magical spot in McCaysville, Georgia, called Delphi University of Spiritual Studies. It's a spiritual center where the most "woo folk" in the world go to become even more "woo."

You know who I'm talking about. "Those people." Like my wife. But in the best way possible. There I was, in the middle of nowhere at Delphi University, taking a program called, "Your Inner Sanctuary." It was me, nine women, and one guy named Asher. We were all sitting on that one sofa your grandma has to have.

The instructor was a festively large woman named Judy. (She would single-handedly fold my brain like a lawn chair and turn me into a quivering and sobbing mess five months after this initial meeting. But that's another story for another time. When you and I meet, ask me about Judy Potter from Delphi. She made it into the Acknowledgments section of this book. What a powerful human!)

Judy led the "Your Inner Sanctuary" program, which was five days long and went from 10:00 am to 7:00 pm with lunch in the middle.

This program was devoted to meditation. The objective was to create a mental sanctuary, a castle inside your mind with various rooms where you can travel to during times of need. I'm sure you've heard the term "compartmentalizing." This is similar. You have eight different rooms inside this mental castle, and you travel to this mind temple to internally build, heal, repair, learn, and receive guidance.

By the end of the program, I'd created my mind map, the internal visualization for what comprises my brain, my thoughts, and my emotional experiences. It was truly a revolutionary few days.

Why am I telling you this story?

Because understanding the relationship with your mind, exploring it, expanding it, tweaking it, adjusting it, and improving it are markers of the best traders that I know. Taking that loss when you need to, holding that winner, embracing times of stress and uncertainty, and knowing and eliminating your weaknesses are key attributes for huge monetary success. That's what you're after, right? It'd better be.

Here are seven legendary steps to *master your mind so you will master the markets.*

1. Do Hard Things

This is imperative! Your definition of "hard" and "things" can vary. Zach Homol (also in my Acknowledgments) is one of the greatest dudes and athletes this planet has to offer. I hired him to help me do hard things harder and better. He began as my ice bath coach. I was terrified of ice baths a few years ago. But the mental edge that emerges, even from one ice bath, is immediately measurable. Your life will be forever changed. Mine certainly was. Do hard things.

I once saw a quote on Instagram that I loved: "I dare you to run a marathon and see if your life doesn't change."

How many people will run a marathon, all 26.2 miles? Less than 4 percent of those on planet Earth.

To date, I've completed over seventy marathons.

I've bear-crawled 3.1 miles, done 40,000+ push-ups in one month, completed three Ironman races, crushed 14,200 jump ropes in a day, knocked out 10,000 push ups in 24 hours, wrote a few best sellers, finished the 29029 Everesting endurance race four times, memorized some Shakespeare, and married a Russian woman. Do hard things.

When you are smack in the middle of doing a hard thing, at some stage it will be just you and your mind. Trading is easy but difficult. Simple but hard. A losing streak is hard. Certain markets can be very tough to navigate. But if you have proven to yourself that you are an overcomer, someone who eventually surpasses all obstacles placed before you, becoming a full-time Real Life Trader is simply one more notch in your belt of greatness!

Doing hard things gives you evidence that you are able to crush any obstacle and hurdle life can throw at you.

2. Learn to Cry and Communicate

Alpha males tend to believe that crying is reserved for the thirteen-year-old in that one movie whose dog died. Men don't cry. Men don't discuss feelings. Men shove everything deep down inside and let it die inside the caverns of their hearts. Right?

Wrong.

Having a healthy relationship with your mind is predicated on your emotional intelligence and awareness.

If you want to be a trader who presses the button and has $100 bills thrown at you daily, you must master your mind. Your mind is you, and when you master yourself, you master the markets.

From both polarities of life, the masculine and the feminine, being able to truly understand, decipher, and then elaborate eloquently what emotions your mind is experiencing and why is a cornerstone for profitability in the markets.

Emotional intelligence empowers individuals to more beautifully experience feelings because individuals become aware of what they are. That awareness leads to the ability to measure, expand, and grow the feelings you want more of while reducing the amount of bad feelings and their frequency of occurrence.

Pro Tip: You become a better person as you understand the emotions your body creates. You also have a shot at being my friend with this skill set. Realistically, the friend of any current or future world leader, nation developer, or fantastic influencer.

3. Meditate Every Now and Then

"In prayer we ask, in meditation we receive."
—Svetlana Newsome

Am I a meditation expert? No. Total logged hours thus far in my journey? Probably two thousand. Inner clarity and awareness is what I'm looking for when I meditate. An opportunity for mental rest. A time to learn, see, hear, and experience my inner journey. Do I engage with it in my daily practice? No. Weekly? Usually. Monthly? Absolutely! Do it when you can, but don't beat yourself up about it.

4. Read New Books and Old Ones

You're already doing this. Great job!

"If you want to succeed, you must read. If you want to lead, you must read. If you want to earn more, you must learn more. The wealthy put their secrets where the poor fail to look. Inside a book."
—Daniel Ally

5. Experience Brand New Things ... Often

New events create new neural pathways in your brain. They tweak, shape, and alter it. This is why I love trading in different locations even inside of my home. Changing it up, mixing up the scenery, even adjusting which side of the bed you sleep on are life alterations that not only are easy and fun but also cause your mind to update! You've updated your software at some point, but how often do you update and upgrade yourself? What version of your mind and body are you on?

6. Give

The fastest way to put your mind and body into an altered state, one created for growth and contribution, is to give generously! When you give, you actively *believe* that you are abundant. When you feel abundant, you focus on the process of the trade and not the money. Thus, you will only get into high probability trades and avoid the need to get into subpar ones.

Find new ways to give. Money is your least valuable asset and the easiest one to donate. So give your knowledge and wisdom. Give your experiences. Give your network and your time. The more creative you are in your giving, the more rewards you'll get from it.

7. Join One of My Trips at www.treesaremoney.com

Peruse that website based on my book *Money Grows on Trees*. See what's up and what dream we are fulfilling. Fun fact: every "Money Grows on Trees" event is a fulfillment of someone else's dream.

In 2019, someone at my event mentioned they'd always wanted to visit Turks and Caicos. In 2021, we did that.

In Turks and Caicos, my best friend, Matt DeLong, mentioned that he wanted to sail the Mediterranean on a yacht.

Three weeks later, the yacht was procured.

In June of 2022, thirty-two friends and I had the adventure of a lifetime sailing the coast of Croatia on a mega yacht. We repeated this life-changing trip in May 2023, and will do it *again* in June 2025.

Be careful what you say out loud around me. My goal in life is to make it happen for you!

CHAPTER 14 :
MASTER RESILIENCE AND
YOU WILL MASTER THE MARKETS

What should you do if you find yourself in the middle of a trading slump?

And by a slump, I don't mean a losing streak of a few trades. I mean, what if you have been so awful for months that you don't even know what a winning streak looks like? You've only had losers. Your profit and loss and your portfolio have been negative from day one.

Pause

The first action step if you're hemorrhaging money? Stop trading.

Wait. Pause. Take a break. Preserve the capital that you have.

Was there ever a point where my trading account resembled a Titanic figurine inside a Hindenburg replica wearing a Detroit Lions jersey handled by the government and then placed inside an egg dropped from a twelve-story building onto a hot concrete sidewalk?

Of course. It happens at least once a year!

At the exact moment I go short, the Federal Reserve prints a few more trillion dollars, the market rallies like crazy, up 10% in five days, and I lose.

Or three days after I buy a bunch of stocks, some leader invades a country, the world panics over a war, the market crumbles, and I lose money.

That's a punch to the gut that's hard for me to shake. Days and weeks fly past, and I'm *not* succeeding.

This happens to everyone and anyone who is super active in the markets.

The good news is that you're doing something drastically wrong; it's your fault, and you're seeing everything incorrectly ... which means you can course correct.

Chances are you're selling low and buying high to then turn around and buy higher to eventually sell lower. You're the mayor of Opposite Land, congratulations.

I know the feeling. I can be a magician at making money disappear. There have been many days where I'm the David Copperfield of the dollar.

What you must do is finger-pound that pause button (as well as that red "Subscribe" button at Real Life Trading on YouTube)!

Beware: Your mind may be yelling, "Hey fool, I'm losing money, and the only way to make it all back is to trade like a rabid animal.

I need to be in everything, all the time, every day in order to make it back."

Your mind is lying to you. Don't dive deeper. Just pause.

Consider this insight from my friend Caryn S.: "The markets are really easy! The broader markets are designed to go up over time. That's why they were created. If you buy pull backs, dips, fear, and recessions, you'll win!"

She's super rich by the way—travels the world, fully retired, living her dream life by spending every month in a new country.

I love her phrase, "designed to go up."

Let that sink in. Essentially, inflation is a guarantee. An asset will cost more and have a larger number attached to it given a big enough time frame.

In theory, increasing your wealth will happen automatically! It's designed to occur. You simply have to take the action, with consistency, and repeat the process of buying that asset.

In my first book, *Money Grows on Trees*, I did my best to make sure that everyone who read it knew to buy AAPL stock. Since I wrote it, AAPL is up 430%. This number will be massively outdated by the time this book is published and then years after that. Bottom line, the returns are astronomical.

Growing money is easy. Expanding your wealth is simple. The hardest part is removing the fear of risk, the fear of failure, the fear of losing it all. Picking your tried and true methods, sticking to them no matter what, and pouring your resources into the direction of abundance is the secret sauce.

Do One Thing Differently

The second action step if your trading account is the Hindenburg is to review your prior trades and find one discernible part of your trading that you can do differently. Comb through your past thirty trades and find one aspect that stands out.

I do this each day I lose and when I have losing weeks. I review every … single … trade.

Did I move my stops too fast? (This is often the problem by the way.)

Yep. I would've had two winners rather than two losers if I hadn't been so scared. So how do I fix that by doing one thing differently? The following week I won't move my stops at all (or I'll move them very slowly, like once an hour).

Fine. I made that single tweak to move my stops slowly. But I'm still lighting Benjamins with kerosine and a match.

Find the Pattern

Now it's time for the third action step.

If I am really bogged down, it's time to find the pattern in the trades.

"A-ha. I'm losing on every bullish trade I take but winning on my bearish ones."

Or "I'm losing on each countertrend trade and winning on all the trades where the trend is easy to see, spot, and determine."

There's always a pattern! You're doing something at the wrong time. Maybe you're shorting dividend paying stocks at fifty-two-week lows?

Maybe you're trading countertrend?

Perhaps you're shorting at or near pre-market lows and buying at or near pre-market highs when day trading?

Look for the pattern! If you need help finding the two or three pebbles in your trading shoes, visit www.reallifetrading.com, and click on the "Mentoring" tab. Hire someone to help you. Work with a market veteran, someone whose primary income is trading, to review why you're sucking eggs.

Wave the White Flag

Since I'm discussing resilience in this chapter, I need to address quitting. When do you throw in the towel? When do you give up on trading?

This is a very valid and real question. Should you have an escape plan? A plan B?

Yes.

There should be a point in every person's life where they go all in. Where Plan A is the only outcome. Burn the boats, take the island, no turning back. Focus on one outcome, winning and finishing, with full resilience, no stopping, only continuation.

But there may also come a point where resilience becomes secondary.

Let me illustrate with a story.

In August 2021, I was going to attempt my first hundred-mile race. Yep, right in the middle of summer. In the state of Georgia. HAWT!

Three weeks before my race, my wife, who's a visionary, woke up one morning at 5:00 am and said, "Don't do this race. I've a really bad feeling. I just had a dream where someone dies in the race." People pay her large sums of money to help them with their dreams, visions, plans, ya know, their future. And this was her advice to me … which I didn't listen to at all. Talk about zero emotional intelligence.

I was like, "Babe, I'm not going to die."

Six days later, one of her spiritual coaches who also is a seer called her from Russia and said, "Tell your husband to be careful in the next few weeks. There's something he is about to embark on that's treacherous."

My wife again asked that I not do the race.

I said, "Babe, I have to. I told the whole world I was going to." I'd even been saying for weeks, "There are only two outcomes of this race: I finish or I die."

Obviously I'm not dead. So what happened?

Eighty-seven miles into the race, my really good friend and pacer Calvin Williams, who had just run seventeen miles with me, said, "Hey man, I'm starting to slow you down. I tweaked my knee. Go ahead to the end of this loop without me and I'll meet you at the camp."

At that point, it was around 9:15 pm, and I'd been up for well over thirty-eight hours.

At mile 89.5, I froze because on the path, about eighteen feet in front of me, were two sleeping black bears. I called my *other* pacer

Christian, and I said, "Hey man, get your truck, and come scare these bears out from in front of me."

Christian arrives in his huge, jacked-up truck with his lights flashing and his horn blaring. And the two smallest black bears in the world run off the path.

Then Christian says, "Hey man, Calvin just called me freaking out. He's lost, and he has no more water or supplies, and I think his phone battery is about to die."

All the things that could go wrong were going wrong. We've all been racing; we're all exhausted; Calvin's lost on some random, amateurly-designed trail with little to no food or water and a dead phone.

Everyone starts flipping out a bit, especially my eight-and-a-half-month-pregnant wife. Oh, did I forget to mention that I dragged a pregnant woman down to one of the hottest places on Earth, where she had to hang out in the heat for hours at a time? God, I suck.

I had to make a decision. For me to finish the last ten and a half miles, we'd need to put all focus and resources on me. But it was raining and dark, and my friend was lost and alone.

The answer was easy. My resilience had to take a back seat.

We drove around all night, honking the horn, yelling, calling the police, fire department, fish and wildlife rescue because my man Calvin's life was on the line. Shit was wild.

But we never found Calvin.

He ended up drinking water from a random stream, "surviving" the

Georgia wilderness through the night, and finding a paved road around around 6:00 am that took him to civilization.

Looking back, it was probably more dramatic than it needed to be. I mean, he's twenty-eight years old and in good health; he was going to be fine for one night until we found him the next morning.

But it could have been worse. And a bullheaded determination to be "resilient" and finish the race would have crossed the line into stubbornness and risky territory.

Sometimes quitting is the opposite of failing. It's necessary, even life-affirming. "Finish or death." When that became an actual reality, I didn't want either. I'm so thankful that Calvin is perfectly fine.

Let me regale you with one more cosmic spin.

Ten years ago, I worked with a couple, Christine and Oliver, who wanted to trade full time. She quit her job at Amazon, sold her Amazon.com, Inc. (AMZN) stock, and both of them went all in on trading.

They had a little north of $200,000 in cash, and they wanted to turn that into $1,000,000 in a year. They knew it was possible but hadn't gotten anywhere by the nine-month mark. So they hired me as a coach. They told me on our first call that they wanted financial freedom and wanted to do it with trading.

For three months, we worked hard on their trading for hours every week. But at the end of those three months, I told them what I tell just 15 percent of the traders I coach: "Trading is not for you."

Why not? Because they refused to follow their rules.

We came up with a rule, "Don't place more than one day trade per day." They broke it within a week. They had the burning desire for success and massive growth that gets many, many traders in trouble. They wanted success too quickly, and they lacked discipline.

They simply had some personality traits that were too deeply rooted for change to occur, at least in trading. I sensed that Christine and Oliver needed something slower, something heavier, something tangible where speed and impulsiveness would not be their downfall.

I guided them into real estate and flipping houses.

Three years later, they had turned their $200,000 into $1,000,000. They became financially free two years after that, and now they flip hotels.

The moral of the story is that trading is amazing and life-changing. It's designed for anyone to win, but not everyone will. Some trees will never grow bananas as much as you might want them to. They're going to produce cherries. Don't cut the tree down just because it doesn't produce bananas!

Everyone who's interested should give trading a shot! Don't be deterred just because you might not win. Learn as much as you can about a subject, and then determine, "Is this right for me?"

Is It Right for Me?

Poker is a good example of this for me.

I'm a top 10 percent poker player in my city. I can consistently play in tournaments, win money, and pull gains at cash games, but it's not my jam.

And I like poker a lot. I studied it like a maniac from thirteen to seventeen years old. But it never was my muse, not like trading is.

Poker never bewitched me like the markets do.

But what if it had?

What if I had dedicated all of my time and energy to playing poker? One of two things would probably have happened.

In the best case, I would've become a master at it. I'd know all of the math; I would've memorized everything about pot odds; I would've been on TV at one of those fancy tournaments; I would've spent loads of time in casinos; and I likely would've made a few million dollars.

The second outcome?

I would've lost money and eventually quit, failed, and given up. That actually doesn't sound horrible to me even now.

But failing in the market? Failing at being a great investor, a prolific trader, and a world-renowned personality that uplifts, enriches, and guides folks through the pitfalls of Wall Street sounds terrifying.

I recently had a profound discussion with some friends about when quitting is the right thing to do.

My answer: Does continuing negatively affect other people?

If pursuing your win, continuing your race, or not slowing down on your journey puts a strain on or directly impacts people in a negative way, it's quit-worthy. If you're creating emotional damage through your actions, you're not living in alignment. It's okay to quit! Failure is a requirement for all success. It's part of the formula. It's the common ingredient in all heroes.

Failure comes with pain, and pain always serves as a motivation, a reminder, a guide, a brochure of what not to do.

Have that discussion with your spouse, family, pastor, best friend, whoever you talk to about doing hard things. Make sure you're not causing pain. And if you are, learn your lesson, take the loss with dignity, become stronger, grow, and then find other ways to create income.

Because you need to *master both resilience and income in order to master the markets.*

CHAPTER 15 :
MASTER PAYTIENCE AND
YOU WILL MASTER THE MARKETS

I love misspelling words meaningfully ... and it's a favorite for the editors.

You get paid when you are "paytient."

The longer a trader can wait, stick to a plan, be cool, calm, and collected, the more profitable that trader will be over the long run.

I've hosted a wildly popular mentorship called "TSLA TITANS" where participants focus only on TSLA for three weeks, which is longer than most individual traders will ever stick to one ticker. When you create an intensity of focus, nuances will be revealed to you.

Participants are wildly "paytient" in this program, waiting for premium set ups and only trading TSLA if it has moved past the prior day's low or the prior day's high.

During this mentorship program, I was asked by a beautiful soul named Indy: "Is there ever a time where you know in advance that you're going to take a bunch of trades because the edge is there and you're in massive flow?"

I'll answer this part of his question first: "Is there ever a time where you know in advance that you're going to take a bunch of trades because the edge is there?"

It all comes down to how much risk I have to appropriate.

For example, if I'm sitting at 3.1R on the month with two days left to trade, I'm going to trade very cautiously. I'll only take A+ setups. When I do take a trade, once I'm around +0.9R, I'll watch it like a hawk until I see any reason to exit. Then I take the 0.9R win so I can lock in my standard of 4R per month.

If I'm down 3.2R on the month, I practice extreme caution and tons of waiting because more active trading will not solve that issue. At -3.2R, I only need two or three trades to be back in the positive, so it becomes a waiting game to see the setup I love.

These two examples together beg the question: Why not *only* always take A+ trades?

Right?! Insert sarcastic grin. ;)

Back to reality where I have some C+ or B- trades because I get antsy with waiting for perfection, then realize the error of my ways afterward.

I can answer for sure, however, that it's very dangerous to go into a trading day expecting to make money, expecting in advance that I'm "going to take a bunch of trades because the edge is there."

"Oh, what a money-making Tuesday this will be! I'm feeling on top of the world. I'm going to take at least five trades, crush them all, and pay for my mortgage" … is the fastest way to light $20,000 on fire in my experience.

Of course you can and should go into a trading day with an "edge."

You certainly can have a system that says, "I'm allowed to take x amount of trades today for y reason." Or, "Per my rules, I can and should trade x stock because of y factor."

That factor, for me, often is the daily gap. Pull up Netflix, Inc. (NFLX) on October 19, 2022. What a great gap that was. Such a strong, easily recognizable bullish gap and go. This edge would have helped you *or anyone* with good chart-reading skills to pre-plan a bullish trade.

Let's look at the second part of Indy's question: "And you're in massive flow?"

You have likely heard this term *flow* before. Everything is easy, simple, and organic. No force.

Here is exactly how I answered Indy's question:

> *Thinking you're in flow is a very dangerous approach, in my opinion. Saying to yourself in advance, 'Oh, I'm in a flow, let me take a hundred trades and make pots of money.' No. The moment when I recognize I'm in pure flow is an entire global circumstance. Everything in my life is easy, simple, without any friction. Money is being thrown at me left and right, health is tremendous, no pain in my body, all of my business relationships are going well, phone calls are easy, and life is exceptional! That's flow for me. And when I feel that, see it, and recognize it, I'm very grateful. In my experience this is a season. This is the time to reap the harvest and enjoy. Buy*

assets, pay down any lame debts, be smart with your money and stack cash.

That was my reply to him in that moment. Word for word.

Perhaps my definition, experience, and understanding of flow will change in the future. Maybe I'll be able to stay in it longer, recognize it earlier, and take advantage of it faster.

I've been in flow many times during seemingly trivial moments like after running, when I have the perfect song on while I'm writing, being engrossed in a great film or sporting event, or spending time hiking with my family.

But being in flow while trading is still a rare event for me.

That said, I am working on helping traders recognize their state of flow. I am partnering with a company that uses brainwave scanning technology to accurately determine when a trader is in the state of flow!

If you want to know more, check out the "Unlocking Optimal Trading: How AI Brainwave Tech Taps into the 'State of Flow'" video on YouTube. Let me know what you think!

CHAPTER 16 :
MASTER CONTINUOUS LEARNING AND YOU WILL MASTER THE MARKETS

You're after trading as a career, right?

You want to do this full time as a job, as a long-term profession?

You made it to Chapter 16; that means you're destined to trade full time!

Everyone else has already given up. They probably threw in the towel during one of my rants in Chapter 3. The gold is always buried deeper than most will dig.

So you've learned my insights on how to start and build your trading for the first four to five years. Now comes the big-hairy-audacious part.

How do you *maintain* success for decades in trading?

Following is the textbook answer from Investopedia regarding the topic "How to stay successful in trading over a twenty-year career?"

Staying successful in trading over a twenty-year career requires dedication, discipline, and focus. Building a solid foundation of understanding of the markets and developing trading techniques that work best for your strategy is essential. Additionally, it's important to use risk management tools such as stop-loss orders and position sizing to limit losses. It's also important to stay up to date on the latest news and trends in the markets so that you can adjust your strategy accordingly. Finally, it's important to remain focused, disciplined, and stay away from impulsive decisions.

Blah, blah. I almost never look at the news. Even when I do, I miss plenty of connections and parallels that seem *so* obvious in hindsight. For example, when the COVID-19 pandemic shut the world down, everyone stayed at home and reorganized their offices by purchasing tons of items from websites like wayfair.com. And ticker W went up 1400% in one year!

I missed out on that glaringly obvious news-based, macroeconomy-squeezed stock trade. Oops.

My whole philosophy in trading liquid markets can be boiled down to this:

Study the technical charts on multiple time frames using a maximum of one indicator along with a maximum of five moving averages to help you determine the trend. Once you find the trend, implement a strategy that'll provide you gains in the direction of the trend while limiting your losses. Exploit the patterns you find using compounding and second-grade math. As you build your profits, pull them out to buy assets that grow exponentially while simultaneously increasing in value and increasing your value as a person!

Remember in Chapter 9 where I mentioned real estate being safe? This is a *great* time to start buying some tangible properties when you have profits to spend!

And now, another giant cliché. Be focused on consistent, never-ending improvement. Always study, learn, read, adapt, and realize that you don't know everything. This approach will help you to continually challenge yourself and push yourself to become even better. Adopting this mindset brings continual growth and development in yourself and your endeavors.

OK. Enough said on that subject.

Indicators

I said in my philosophy to use a maximum of one indicator.

Which indicators are the best? Do individuals ever create new ones that are actually useful and relevant?

Absolutely.

Is there a *magic indicator* where all you do is crush it and constantly win every single day?

No.

One of my favorite hobbies is practicing different indicators and scanning through how I would've entered and exited. I journal my performance and then pick a new stock and new indicator and go to battle! Or I backtest the same stock/asset class versus numerous different indicators.

One indicator I really do love is Relative Strength Index, or RSI.

I use it to find divergence, both bullish and bearish, or to determine if a trend is too hot for the bears or bulls and needs to rest.

You can find some excellent charts illustrating RSI in the free PDF handbook at www.reallifetrading.com/master-yourself that you can download by entering your name and email (pay particular attention to Figures R.S, A.B, and B.D).

Another indicator I enjoy a lot is Moon Phases on TradingView. Play with that one a bit. You'll be blown away!

I've made videos on both of these indicators for you to check out. On YouTube, search for "RSI Indicator Real Life Trading" and "Moon Phases Real Life Trading."

TikTok also has a lot of videos of people sharing their indicators; I've probably watched at least ten hours' worth.

Real Life Trading has a few of its own, which we have built and automated into robotic trading systems.

Here is my #1 rule with indicators: If you have them on your screen, use them. Otherwise, you're wasting time, effort, and space on your charts. There's very little point in using an indicator that says "SELL" in big red letters on your chart only for you to ignore it.

Beyond Indicators

What else helps traders maintain success long term?

I reached out on X to four of my trading buddies, mentors, and coaches and asked.

The common answers were risk management and continuous learning!

First up is Dennis Dick's response:

Jerremy Newsome: What's your advice on "how to stay successful in trading as a 20 year career?"

Dennis Dick: Constantly adapting your strategies to the trading environment.

Jerremy Newsome: Does that mean learning new ones or tweaking old ones?

Dennis Dick: Both.

Per Dennis, it's crucial to study multiple trading strategies. The markets frequently fluctuate and change; therefore, you should have the capacity to be equally flexible. A bullish strategy like "put sales" will cause you to go bankrupt in a strong down-trending market environment like that of 2021 and 2022.

Having the capacity to understand both long and short trades, along with directional trading and non-directional trading, is paramount. There are times in the market where it's going to be correcting, chopping, trading sideways; essentially *not* trending. In this environment, option trading, day trading, and channel trading may be the only systems that work.

When the trend resumes, it's safe to say the best strategies to employ will be the ones that follow that trend and make the most money in that direction.

Next, here comes my boy Pete discussing discipline!

Jerremy Newsome: What is your advice on "how to stay successful in trading as a 20 year career?"

Pete Najarian: Always discipline on good & bad investments/trades.

Now Pete is one of those 5:00 am, treadmill-and-StairMaster-everyday kind of dudes. His discipline is in his routines.

My take on his statement is that, *initially*, you won't know which trades or investments will be winners or losers. So the best approach is to treat them all the same—not doubling down, not allowing fear and emotions to wreck your success in life.

Heck, discipline's really the secret to anything in life. Have that unwavering, unshakable consistency to grind, repeat, and produce greatness through your day-to-day routines and the mental fortitude to not cave into the fear that will inevitably reveal itself.

Brian and Christian both mention risk management.

> *Jeremy Newsome: What is your advice on "how to stay successful in trading as a 20 year career?"*

> *Brian Shannon: Manage risk aggressively, market doesn't care what we think should happen.*

> *Christian Fromhertz: Risk management, developing your own trading plan/system, and adapting to the market you are in.*

I covered risk management in Chapters 5 and 6 where I discussed the R system and trading plans. Knowing your risk, keeping it consistent, and understanding how to use it is as important as your toothbrush. My target reader for this book brushes their teeth *pretty frequently*.

Risk mitigation to me means keep your money around. Be liquid. You already know how frustrating the markets can be. But there's a time where it *clicks*. You begin to see the patterns and the set ups; you finally begin to plan your trade ahead of time and know precisely what you'll do in any given situation when your emotional self is far less terrified to pull the trigger.

Risk mitigation, asset creation, cash flow production, budgeting, and proper money spending are paramount for long-term wealth and success. These are your essential keys to trading as a profitable career!

CHAPTER 17 :
MASTER STRATEGIES AND YOU WILL MASTER THE MARKETS

Here it is, the *crème de la crème*. Everyone's favorite chapter in any stock book. "Tell me how to make money, Newsome!"

Ok, here goes.

If there's one thing I'm good at, it's creating blueprints for individuals to make more money. I love strategies along with the determination and focus required to know when to adjust them, update them, use them, implement them, and, of course, throw them in the garbage for a while.

The 10 EMA

The first strategy I'll cover took the trading world by storm in 2022. I call it the 10 Exponential Moving Average, or 10 EMA, where 10 is the period of time. This one is pretty uncomplicated. My Real Life Trading YouTube channel offers plenty of videos on this strategy; simply search "10 EMA Real Life Trading," and you'll get your fill.

What's exciting about this strategy is that it can be effectively used on all time frames and on all asset classes. I like to say that, "everything works, just not all the time." This is even more applicable in the trading world. I'll show you below many instances where this strategy works and others where it doesn't.

There are certain instances where this strategy can and does work better than others. I'll do my best to outline those as well.

Go through these strategies and begin building and creating your own. Know that for an extremely large sum of traders, the best path is to create a plan with rules that are easy to explain. Here's an example.

In my 10 EMA strategy, I look for:

- The first bear candle to close above the 10 EMA for a bullish trade or
- The first bull candle to close below the 10 EMA for a bearish trade.

Slide back into www.reallifetrading.com/master-yourself, and, if you haven't yet done so, enter your name and email to download your free PDF handbook for the following charts.

In Figure 2A in your handbook, you'll notice a daily chart of TSLA with the 10 EMA and candles.

Figures 2.1 through 2.4 in the PDF handbook are based on this very chart, but those go forward in time to show when you would've known to set the trade up based on this strategy.

When you play this strategy, it "resets" when you get a candle close past the moving average without triggering. So, once you have a bull candle close below the moving average, your plan is to enter bearish below that bull candle with a stop loss above the 10 EMA.

Look at Figure 2.1 in your handbook. It shows the first bull candle closing below the 10 EMA. Once that candle closes, you'll plan to short (go bearish) *only if price action* goes lower than the low of the bull candle.

This strategy is a momentum play. Either bulls lose money and the stock drops (in the above bull scenario) or the bears are forced to buy to cover, and the stock rips, as in Figure 2.2.

Figure 2.2 shows TSLA making a lower low, but you're eventually going to exit/get stopped out as TSLA breaches past the 10 EMA. Then the next candle that comes in is the first bear candle closing above the 10 EMA. So that was a losing bearish 10 EMA trade.

Figure 2.3 is a bullish 10 EMA entry. You had the first bearish candle closing above the 10 EMA, so you set up a bullish entry to enter above the high of the bear candle. The bears here get squeezed out, and the stock price is pushed higher because the bear traders are forced to buy to cover.

Next is Figure 2.4. You can see that the bullish trade would have worked very nicely.

A few days later, the strategy resets and you begin looking for the next bear candle to close above the 10 EMA *or* bull candle to close below, whichever happens first. In this instance, on Figure 2.4, it's a nice size bull candle that comes in and closes below the average, which means you will set up a short to go bearish *if* you go lower than the low of that candle. This represents another profitable trade exiting for 1.2 risk units.

Now that you have hit your target and TSLA is at a prior support, you wait! What are you waiting for?

The stock to close above the 10 EMA. And then, you'll wait for either a bear candle to close above or a bull candle to close below. And then you repeat that process for eternity! HAHA.

Let's do two more examples.

The first will be a smaller time frame and a different stock. I'll randomly select NKE.

Look at Figure 3.1, Nike (NKE) on a 3-minute chart.

One of my favorite aspects of technical analysis is the fractal patterns of human emotion and sentiment. If any candle theory and strategy works on a weekly chart, it'll work on a 1-minute chart.

Let's go candle by candle on Figure 3.1. The first two candles of this move right at market open are quite bullish. Strong move, solid volume, both closing above the 10 EMA. At this stage, once those bull candles come in and close above the moving average, it would be appropriate to plan for a bear candle to come in. Sure enough, the third candle of the day is a bear candle closing above the 10 EMA. You'd have set up your long entry to get in above the high and stop below the 10 EMA.

The *next* candle that comes in *also* closes above the 10 EMA. It's also a bearish candle, and the high of that candle is lower than the high of the third candle. In this situation, you'd have lowered your entry and, sure enough, no trigger once again.

The fifth candle in this sequence is a large bearish candle closing below the 10 EMA. This resets "the count," which is where you wait for a bull candle to close below the moving average or another bear candle closing above the moving average.

The sixth candle on this move does close below the moving average, and it's a bullish candle, which means you would've set up a bearish entry to get in below the low of that candle and stop above the average. Once again, no trigger.

As this stock progresses, you can see the bull candle that does close below the moving average, giving you a glorious set up. Your stop loss would have been above the 10 EMA while simultaneously above the high of the large bearish candle (the fifth candle in this sequence).

I have marked on the chart a bear candle that closes above the 10 EMA. The price action never breached the high of that candle, which would have led to a non-trigger. You'll notice that this happens very often in this strategy, which is great! Non-triggers lead to certainly *not* losing money, which is always the goal.

Look at Figure 4.1, the last chart using the 10 EMA.

I use this one for analysis on a bearish swing trade done on YETI Holdings, Inc. (YETI).

This is a classic example of risking $3 to make $5.

Say your R is $1,000. You'd have shorted 1,000/(37 - 34) = 333 shares, and you'd have bought to cover those shares at a profit at $29.

This represents a 1.5R trade. The reason I share this is because if trading was done with a $5,000 risk, this would have come out to a profit of $7,500, which is enough to buy your whole team YETI coolers as holiday presents!

Day Trading

I wouldn't specifically say that day trading is a strategy as much as it's a time frame and a perspective of trading, but there are certain times where it works exceedingly well compared to other approaches.

Therefore, I'll deem it as a strategy enough to discuss it.

Day trading, as I see it, is awareness and understanding of the daily chart along with the sentiment of the prevailing trend. According to that explanation, day traders should know when the trend can change, even if only momentarily, and take advantage of it.

Day trading is getting into a position and then out of a position on the same day. My day trading goal is two hours per day, four days a week, or approximately two hundred days a year.

I tell newer traders all the time that $200 per day on average x 200 days a year = $40,000 extra side hustle income each year. And, of course, the numbers can scale over the years into something like $4,000 per day on average x 200 days a year = $800,000.

I really do love day trading because you're in cash every night; you're not concerned with the news; and you don't care which direction something moves as long as it just moves. Your goal is to crunch second-grade math, follow your system, be bored, lose small, win big, and trade patterns.

There are no emails, customer service, phone calls, traffic, refunds, toilets, tenants, termites, invoices, tires, oil, grease, bad weather, good weather, mosquito bites, or poison ivy.

With something to trade on and a decent connection or Wi-Fi, you can day trade! You can access the markets and use them as an ATM or an expensive therapist who will show you every day what internal beliefs you hold, what battles you'll face, and what you need to heal in order to become truly exceptional and ridiculously profitable.

Here are the main aspects I analyze and review for a day trade:

1. Large gaps on daily chart [4–20%]

2. Small gaps on daily chart [2–4%]
3. Micro gaps on daily chart [0.5–2%]
4. A price action move above the prior high of day
5. A price action move below the prior low of day

If one of these five things is not happening, I will not take a trade.

I often focus on one stock on any given day. As I've mentioned before, I can have only one stock on my watch list (usually TSLA) and be perfectly content. However, if my TSLA isn't doing #1 to #3 above or hasn't done a #4 or #5 (i.e., TSLA is on an inside day), I'll go find another stock that's gapping #1 or #2 and trade that.

My favorite gaps are simply those where the stock is opening above a prior high of day or below the prior low of day.

My second-favorite gaps are when the stock is opening below the prior bullish candle's open or when the stock is opening above the prior bearish candle's open.

Gaps are very important because they create momentum and spicy moves where bulls and bears are in sheer panic and excitement. This is how you get paid. Capitalize on those situations and keep the money protected.

Example time. Look at Figure 5.1 on your follow-along PDF.

This chart has numerous great gaps to choose from. I selected four at random, but I could study this chart for hours.

The way I began to understand *sentiment* and how traders feel is by looking at a chart, knowing it comprises real people, and asking the question, "How do the prior traders feel with this stock opening here?"

In this first arrow on the left in Figure 5.1, the trend is slightly bearish. And then suddenly a beautiful open occurs above the high of the prior day and above the high of quite a few candles. The bulls get very excited, but only for two days, and the bears slowly regain their control of this trend. But that gap scared them! If you were day trading that day, I think it would have been easy to identify their fear and play that move bullishly.

On the second arrow, the bears are trying to stay in control. The trend made a lower low, and the bears want to ensure another low high happens. However, there are four small, sideways days where buyers and sellers are bored of battling. Eventually there's a victor, and it's the zealous buyers! The stock opens above the high of those four small days, and opens above the prior day's high as well. This is a gap I call a bullish gap-and-go.

The third arrow is similar to the first in that you have a bullish candle on the prior day with a decent upper shadow, and the stock is opening above the high of the prior day. The trend is already decidedly bullish as the stock opens above every candle on the screen. Stay long, buy the dip.

And then—the fourth arrow—first-degree murder.

A great display of fear, panic, and despair as the sellers chase down any buyers with a pitchfork. The stock opens down in gargantuan fashion trapping any and all prior buyers, which is why so much selling took place on this day. A wonderful opportunity to short.

Now on Figure 6.1, you'll zoom into a 3-minute chart of that gap down on the intraday price action on December 30, 2022.

Knowing the predominant sentiment should be fear and selling, a great trade would have appeared for anyone who was "paytient" enough to play it!

Often when I day trade the price action breaking past high of day or low of day, I'm playing support or resistance style setups. Figure 7.1 and Figure 8.1 are two additional examples of buying low at support and selling high at resistance for two day trade set ups.

The style of trading shown in Figures 7.1 and 8.1 can be very scary for newer traders because it offers very little "confirmation" that the trade will move in the desired direction. I cannot emphasize enough how beneficial it is to practice this approach especially if the pre-market low/support is close to the *prior low of day*. I get really excited about buying off of those levels. And vice versa; if the pre-market resistance is also near the prior high of day, I'll short.

As mentioned in previous chapters, I always go into this trade knowing, planning, and preparing to lose. I'm setting up for 1.2R of profit (1.2 x the stop value), and I expect to move my stop from -1R loss to -0.7R loss after thirty minutes of being in the trade.

When day trading, I follow a couple of rules regarding stop movement:

1. If I'm bullish, I never move my stop on a bear candle (this shows fear and no pre-planning).
2. If I'm bearish, I never move my stop on a bull candle (this shows fear and no pre-planning).

So I wait for the candle to move in my direction before I move my stop. And then, every twenty to thirty minutes, I move my stop -1R, -0.7R, -0.5R, -0.2R, then profitable.

The only way to hold a winning trade is to practice holding trades. You must build that holding muscle methodically and consistently. I aim to exit at 1.2R on my day trades until I hit 6R for the month. After I have secured a net profit (so far) for the month (if I hit this, it's usually around the 20th of the month), I know I have six to eight trading days left where I can stretch my targets into 1.5R to 1.8R. If I hit 10R for the month, I begin to shoot for 2R to 2.4R on my targets. When you win, win big; when you lose, lose small! That's the formula for success in this game.

As mentioned previously on the NKE example, the 10 EMA strategy works well intraday as well!

I've noticed the 10 EMA strategy works best between 10:15 and 15:35 Eastern Time.

Look at Figure 9.1 in your handbook.

In Figure 9.1, there are three stunning setups on NVIDIA Corporation (NVDA) using the 10 EMA shown with the black arrows.

The 3-minute chart is my preferred day trade time frame. I do like trading from the 2-minute chart occasionally, especially if it's a spectacular gap nice and early in the morning. I've messed around with the 4-minute chart some. It's kind of cool!

I used to trade the 5-minute chart as my main time frame, but I felt like it became too slow. I'll still browse through it every so often, usually after I'm in a trade and I want a slower pace to calm my nerves.

With the markets, you have endless day trading strategies, tips, and ways to approach this time frame. The best way is to create a focus, something you master for a period of time.

Here are some of the strategies:

- Stocks gapping down that you're going to play bullish as a fade.
- Stocks gapping down that you're going to short, playing the trend.

- Only day trading TSLA.
- Looking only to play gap ups but being able to play them in any direction.
- Playing only gap downs on TSLA.

Any strategy, style, and approach can be used in day trading, but the greatest life hack is focusing on one particular discipline for one to three months so you feel extremely comfortable when the opportunity arises to trade that style of move.

The Collar Strategy

The collar strategy is my favorite strategy. When you talk about safety, security, passive investing, and making money while you sleep, I think of the collar strategy.

It's also my rabbit in the hat at dinner parties when I'm trying to be a magician of the markets. And that's because it's a strategy *most* humans don't know about. I have shocked many strikingly wealthy business owners, real estate investors, and stock-holding participants with the simplicity of the collar.

I have a course on www.reallifetrading.com called "Hedging with Options" that takes this strategy to a different dimension of excellence. If you find yourself in a position where you have more than $100,000 invested in the markets, this is the best course you'll ever take on options.

If you want more bite-sized information, search "Collar Strategy Real Life Trading" on YouTube, and watch all of those videos.

In essence, the collar is a limited return, limited risk strategy that uses options as they were created to be used: super cool insurance contracts. Brace yourself, fourth-grade math is coming. If you are unfamiliar with option trading, make sure you pop over to www.reallifetrading.com, and take our classes on options! It will change your life!

I'll use a written example and a chart example to illustrate.

If you buy stock XYZ at $50 and the stock increases in value from $50 to $60, you have a $10 value gain in equity. This is the stage where it's best and most conducive to implement a collar. You would do that by selling a $65 call option and hopefully buy a $50 put option. The expiration on the call and the put are usually the same. Say for clarity's sake that this is a thirty-five-day sold call and a thirty-five-day bought put. The sold call would probably bring in a $1.25 credit, and the put option would be a total debit of around $0.90. That means that the overall net credit on this trade is $0.35 per share.

This gives you the capacity to sell your shares at either $50 for break-even or $65 for a profit. For thirty-five days (the length of expiration on both contracts), this trade becomes extremely favorable! Realistically the shares are protected from any loss for thirty-five days. You either lose nothing or make 25% return on investment (ROI) on your shares. Yes, seriously.

WHHHATTT?! Yes! Seriously, how cool?!

Collars, and specifically option selling, is how billionaire stock owners make silly money annually. Obviously they don't want to sell their shares, which means they'll not be using stop losses. So they sell calls and use that premium to buy *free* puts. And this can create win-win scenarios to generate additional cash flow for those shareholders/owners/CEOs even if the stock doesn't pay dividends. The more you know, right?

Often, the hardest challenge of the collar is buying the shares at the right location, being "paytient" enough to wait for the shares to increase in value, and then selling the call and buying the put.

If you're buying into a position and you immediately want to get into a collar, it becomes very challenging to create a favorable position.

For example, stock XYZ is bought at $50. At the exact moment of buying the stock, the investor buys a $45 put option for a thirty-five-day expiration and sells a $55 thirty-five-day expiration call option, giving the investor a 10% win possibility or a 10% loss possibility. There's a very large chance this exact trade would *cost* money as well, resulting in an overall debit and not a credit like above.

So I've learned this about collars:

This is a strategy I'll implement with over $10,000,000 on a singular stock, no problem with no fear, but only *after the stock has gained in positive equity*. Let's review a recent trade on Pinterest, Inc. (PINS). This will be covered through Figures 11.1 and 12.1 on the free PDF handbook available at www.reallifetrading.com/master-yourself.

Look at Figure 11.1.

I bought PINS at a previous price in 2020. I began buying shares around $22 per share and the trade/investment/swing trade worked out really well. Therefore, it made sense to begin doing it again. You'll notice in Figure 11.1 that higher lows were beginning to form. The stock was above its 100/200 simple moving average (SMA) on the daily chart. They previously acted as a resistance and were now acting as a support (potentially). I was buying at $22.72, knowing that my exit would be $20. So my initial risk was only $2.72 per share. My risk per trade was $5,000 in 2022; therefore, I bought 5000/2.72 = 1838 shares (I rounded up to 2,000 shares).

Take a look at Figure 12.1.

Guess what happens five trading days later?

Randomly, the overall markets had a hugely bullish day. PINS popped gorgeously and perfectly! It was as though I had scripted this. In the chart, you'll see huge buying volume come in at that prior resistance. This is three bullish buying days in a row; PINS is up 16% from where I bought it, a dream come true!

So, what do I implement? A collar!

On December 13, 2022, I sold a $28 January 20, 2023 call option and simultaneously purchased a $24 January 20, 2023 put option. This trade resulted in a *net credit* of $0.22 *per share.*

And $0.22 x 2,000 shares = $440. I got paid $440 on this collar to either win 5.6% (selling at $24) or *win* 23.2% (selling at $28).

WHHHATTT?!
YYYYEESSS!!

That's why I'm saying this strategy is extraordinary. On that third Friday of January 2023, one of three results was going to occur: if PINS was below $24, I'd let it auto-sell my shares there for my gain; if it was above $24 and below $28, then I'd do this trade *again* for February or March and get paid another net credit; or if PINS was above $28, I'd sell my shares and look to get in again later.

LETS GOOOOO!!!

And that's the collar. How cool, right?! You make your money when you buy. Getting into the shares at the best price is the key to this strategy working out flawlessly. I do use my long-term averages to help me time my entry with the collar because it's one I like to do with size! I'll pull up the 100/200 SMA daily, weekly, and even monthly and browse where it's at to determine my entry. In fact, I use those moving averages for a lot of my strategies; I'll further discuss them later in this chapter.

The delightful aspect of collars is that they can be used in a short/bearish position too.

If you're bearish, you sell the stock short, buy call options as the upside insurance/protection, and sell puts to bring in your premium to pay for the call purchase.

Here are some quick tips that'll help you with your collars.

You want to sell your calls and buy your puts after three or more up days. You'll get more premium for the calls and pay less money for the puts.

If you're playing a short collar, this is reversed. You want to sell your puts after three or more down days and buy your calls.

I try my absolute best to sell the same expiration on both the call and the put. But there can be some excellent opportunities where you might not have to. This depends on your cost basis for the shares. To gain more insight on the when/where/why/how of collars, check out that "Hedging with Options" program. It totally slaps!

Credit Spreads

Now this is an interesting strategy. It can be a brilliant approach to a market where you don't know exactly what it's doing, but you have a decent consensus on what it *shouldn't do.*

What the heck does that mean?

Well, with credit spreads, the trader uses the power of options to create income and cash flow by simply analyzing, choosing, determining, processing, and kind of betting on where a stock will not go and when.

Let's peek into charts real quick.

You'll look at three different credit spreads on three very different assets.

The first credit spread covered is called a bear call spread, and you'll set it up on SPDR Dow Jones Industrial Average ETF Trust (DIA) represented by Figure 13.1.

A bear call spread is a bearish position where a trader makes the evaluation that a stock will not go past a certain level on a certain date. You get *paid* to make this determination in the form of a credit. The process is quite simple for a bear call spread. You sell a call option and buy a higher call option with the same expiration date.

Look at Figure 13.1.

The DIA is actually an ETF (exchange-traded fund), not a stock specifically. This is the best and easiest way for the general public to trade the actual Dow Jones Industrial Average. One can buy, own, and actively trade what's lovingly referred to as the Diamonds.

On the trade shown in Figure 13.1, many option traders at Real Life Trading sold a $350 December 23, 2022 call option and simultaneously bought a $355 December 23, 2022 call option. This resulted in a $0.65 credit per contract.

Since my risk was $5,000 in 2022, I sold ten of these contracts. I brought $650 in cash flow on this trade. This represents a 13% return on risk. Credit spreads are a high probability, low return, larger risk, higher chance of winning type of strategy. In proper market environments, they can also be a lot of fun. I work with hundreds of traders who make absurd money using this strategy, especially on the S&P 500 (SPX) selling three-day and zero-day expiration credit spreads.

Now look at Figure 14.1. It shows the time and price action when I was losing on this credit spread *even though* the price itself was not above $350.

This particular bear call spread was showing a negative profit and loss (PnL) (as all bear credit spreads will) as the DIA went higher. It was showing a loss (on paper) from November 10 to November 30. However, the DIA was still four points lower than my sold call even at its highest on November 30. And that's what I love about credit spreads. It's a math- and timing-style strategy, which usually allures my engineers and math nerds. This trade will win unless the DIA closes above $350 on December 23 in this example. It's an absolute guarantee that you'll win on this trade if anything other than the above occurs.

So even though I was down on this spread for a while, time was on my side. All I had to do was wait. Notice on the chart, the DIA had rallied from October, when it was around $290 a share, to $331 when I sold the call spread. That was a 15% bull move. And from valley to peak, the DIA was up 20% from October 13, 2022 to November 30, 2022, which is ... a lot! So my thought was simple. The DIA is going to get some selling, some consolidation, rest, and pull back *at some point*. And, as you can see, it did. I won on this credit spread simply by selecting the perspective that the DIA could rally and continue higher, but not *that* high, *that* fast.

Figure 15.1 shows another bear call spread that I really loved.

On December 1, 2022, AAPL was trading below its 100/200 SMA on the daily, and it was running into the 100 SMA on the weekly as well. Double resistance! Plus AAPL overall, with the rest of the markets, was in a down trend, making lower lows and lower highs. Looking at this chart, you can probably see how well AAPL respected and eventually failed the 100/200 SMA in November. The main aspect of most of my trading is *what did the stock do last time this occurred?*

121

Make sure you look at other time frames and other moving averages because it is really useful on this trade as well.

Figure 16.1 shows the weekly chart of AAPL during the time I was setting up this trade.

I used it to determine if the price action of AAPL was:

1. In a down trend on a weekly (making lower highs).
2. Below the 100 SMA on a daily chart.
3. Below the 200 SMA on a daily chart.
4. Below the 100 SMA on a weekly chart.
5. Below the 10/20/50 exponential moving averages on a weekly chart.

And if:

6. I was able to get over a 10% return on risk from my credit spread.
7. I was able to sell less than six weeks of time.

With all of those check marks, I sold a $155/$160 December 23, 2022 bear call spread on AAPL when AAPL was trading at $148. I got paid $0.55 for this spread, just a hair above 10%, which is the minimum I'm looking to earn per spread.

AAPL chopped around, traded sideways to down for a few weeks, and the spread expired, worthless. Boom, easy money.

The above analysis took me roughly two to three minutes. And this process can be repeated easily, quickly, and often.

When you get time, head over to www.reallifetrading.com to take our credit spread course, and dive into our videos on YouTube by searching credit spreads on the Real Life Trading channel. Our mission is to enrich lives! Enjoy that content.

Let's investigate another style of credit spread—this one is for my bulls! For the traders who want to collect a high probability pay day by allowing the stock to bounce, go up, trade sideways, rip higher, or go down just a little.

This example is shown in Figure 17.1.

Figure 17.1 shows a daily chart of NFLX. The bear gap down occurred on December 15, 2022. NFLX had a pretty large down day with a strong gap. Go look at this on a chart. You will notice, on that day, NFLX was down an intimidating 9%. Fear was creeping in; this was the second down day in a row and the fifth bearish candle in a row. In other words, my assumption was that you'd get some buying at some point.

I love using 100 and 200 SMAs on all my charts and the three major time frames: daily, weekly, and monthly. Notice the 100 SMA on a monthly chart was below the stock price, meaning it would, hopefully, and likely, act as a support. NFLX being at $290 here, the 100 SMA on a monthly at $278, the 100 SMA on a daily at $256, and the 200 SMA on a daily at $251 gives you easily six to seven check marks of verification and information. You can also see NFLX was in a bullish uptrend, making higher highs and higher lows.

Again, the cool part of this strategy is that while I wasn't confident enough to buy shares or buy a call option on NFLX, I noticed that the stock had numerous moving averages acting as a support, which helped me conclude that NFLX would not speedily crash down below $250, which was 14% away.

With all of this information at my disposal, I sold the January 13, 2023 $250/$245 bull put spread.

This style of credit spread is bullish because you're selling a put. It's protected because you buy a lower strike put which acts as insurance for the insurance you sold to someone else. In the real world, this is called *reinsurance*, which is a very real thing!

For the $250 sold put and the $245 bought put, my credit on that trade ended up being $0.55, very similar to my AAPL credit spread. If you're good with dates and times, you'll notice that I was in both AAPL and NFLX at the same time. One bullish position (NFLX) and one bearish position (AAPL), both on large-name technical stocks.

I feel like this was a *professional* move because it shows neutrality and a high degree of scanning capability, always looking for an opportunity. *Finding* the deal in the markets is the easiest part! The deals are on any given ticker all the time. Some are certainly better than others, and you'll get paid to find them.

As I wrote this book, I was still in this NFLX bull put spread. I expected to be able to buy to close this spread on January 3, 2023 for 80% capture of my premium, or to just set an alert at $260 (below the daily 100 SMA) and close the spread if NFLX got that low, which was unlikely at that point. As you read this, check to see where NFLX closed on January 13, 2023. My guess was $293.72, which meant NFLX will have closed above $250 and this bull put spread will have gone to options heaven. Figure 18.1 shows the daily chart of NFLX as I hammered this book out on my keyboard.

Make sure to get more education on credit spreads from Real Life Trading. We are exceptional at properly implementing these tools and strategies because we, as a team, company, and movement live, eat, and breathe this stuff!

Some rules for credit spreads:

1. Make sure you're selling your puts or your calls after multiple days in a row of price action.

2. Don't try to pick an all-time high sell off using bear call spreads.
3. Don't try to pick an all-time low bottom using bull put spreads.
4. Use your moving averages on all major time frames (daily, weekly, monthly) to track down the most check marks possible to increase your odds of winning.
5. Realize there are specific tools to implement at specific times! I don't get into a credit spread just to gain or earn income that week even if I need it badly. Waiting is always greater than diving into something because I'm bored.
6. I aim for 10–15% return on my spreads.
7. If I can buy to close any option for a 50% premium capture within a week of the sale, I do.
8. If I can buy to close any option for a 75% premium capture if more than two weeks remain on expiration, I do.

As with anything, there are always nuances, updates, and specific set ups that intrigue me more than others. But I'd love for you to master credit spreads and other option selling strategies so you feel very comfortable and confident when you can, should, and are able to implement them.

Debit Spreads

The last specific strategy is debit spreads. Of all the strategies discussed in this book, this is my least frequently used.

I get into debit spreads when I'm not confident of the trend. There's rarely good momentum in play, but usually there's a compelling chart pattern, often a large head and shoulders, where I feel like the stock *should* tank, but I want to limit my downside.

For example: If you see stock XYZ might get crushed, and you expect a large move lower, you're going to get puts, right?

Say the stock is at $100. And you buy a $100 put for four-months expiration. That put might cost you $8 per contract.

Well, if you also sell an $80 put, you'll *bring in premium (credit)*, which will dramatically reduce the cost of your risk exposure. Say, as an example, that this option brings in $1.50. Your total net debit would be $6.50 and your maximum gain is $100 - $80 - $6.50 = $13.50. So you'd risk $6.50 to possibly make $13.50. Not too terrible.

An example of a debit spread I implemented was a $75/$105 February debit spread on Digital World Acquisition Corp. (DWAC). See Figure 19.1 in your handbook.

You'll notice it had a bullish 10 EMA setting up (which was a bear candle closing above the 10 EMA). The debit spread cost, in total, $2.80.

With any trade, debit spreads being no different, you can place a stop loss. But you don't *have to* since it's very easy to calculate your risk with a debit spread. If the trade doesn't run higher, goes down, or goes sideways, your max loss is $2.80 per contract.

And, in this example, $105 - $75 - $2.80 = $27.20. This was a 10:1 risk-reward set up.

Debit spreads are also semi-cool because if you get into them and the position does begin to form a nothing burger, you can always spend additional money and buy to close the sold option, uncapping your position just in case it does run. I didn't do this on the DWAC trade, although it would have been nice.

Debit spreads for me are very often a trade where nothing is happening yet, but a news event, earnings, or something is approaching, and I want to reduce my actual cost of being in.

This debit spread is known as a bull call spread, namely because you're bullish, you want the stock to go higher, and you're using calls.

The other debit spread is known as a bear put spread. This one is when you're bearish and you want the stock to drop.

Figure 20.1 is the follow-up for DWAC.

It did end up running a bit, and I sold my debit spread, which you can do just like any other position. When you exit a spread, either debit or credit, you'll need to close both legs together. This is the part that requires practice. The opening and closing of spreads!

Option strategies are why paper trading was invented. In my opinion, there's really no need to *paper trade* stocks. You buy them or sell them. Once you learn what the buttons do in the broker (and perhaps you've paper traded for one to three weeks), dive in with a small risk and get started.

But options are "a whole new world," as Aladdin says. Many books have been written focusing solely on option strategies: how to get in, how to get out, how to play defense, and when to really level up and play offense.

And I've read a lot of those books. Trust me, they're boring. I believe the best way to learn option strategies is by looking at charts, videos, option chains, and paper trading them for a few weeks or even months. See how they move, adjust, and update; become familiar with the bid/ask spreads; and know how to set up advanced orders—all the goodies!

At Real Life Trading, we are always available, happy, willing, and able to hold anyone's hand and show you how to use these incredible features to revolutionize your portfolio and finances.

To get more strategies, information, insight, or thoughts on the markets, head over to www.reallifetrading.com to get hours of free training and education.

CHAPTER 18 :
MASTER LONG-TERM STOCK SELECTION AND YOU WILL MASTER THE MARKETS

There'll never be another AAPL. But there doesn't have to be. There'll be other companies that create similar explosive growth opportunities. Will they be in tech? Will they create insane fandom? Will they divide the world into the haves and have-nots who use AAPL products? Who knows. I can say, however, that AAPL did phenomenally well as a company.

Next, I'll outline some other companies I believe will have ridiculous returns over the next ten years, and I'll tell you why.

I mean, what type of trading book would this be without some stock picks? Of course, some (many?) stock picks will undoubtedly be outdated in a decade. Thanks to mergers and acquisitions, marketplace changes, restructuring, divorces, and global market changes, everything will shift and be altered. My picks are simply my opinions and not financial advice of any kind.

More importantly, however, what type of psychological mastery book would this be if I didn't discuss how to hold a winner along with the steps and actions and research that needs to take place?

First, my picks.

My approach is to outline what made AAPL successful and try to reverse engineer that. Add some components of culture, vision, trendiness, need of use, purpose, growth, positive earnings, a great leadership team, and a touch of luck and I see what shakes out.

I'll go with larger companies first, the ones that *already made it* and will still offer sound bullish trends for investing in the next twenty years. Companies that I believe have broken through to *the other side* where 20–50% per year trading potential, both up and down, is extremely likely and foreseeable to me.

Companies like ADBE, NFLX, MSFT, INTU, ORCL, NKE, SBUX, PG, JNJ, PFE, COST, WMT, YUM, TMUS, AZO, ORLY, CAT, GOOGL, AMZN, MNST, AFL, V, MA, JPM, GS, and MGEE will offer extremely fun trading and longer-term buy and hold opportunities along with the obvious AAPL. These are stocks that I often throw into the "they'll likely be around for a very long time" category, which allows me to still want to buy the stock as low as I can and sell it as high as possible, but I'm comfortable doing so with a larger size. Can these stocks still have dramatic, 50+% bearish corrections and pull backs? Absolutely!! Will they? Probably. Some already have. But I believe larger pull backs on the above companies are great times to protect capital with the collar strategies I discussed in the prior chapter.

Following is a list of explosive stocks that will have wild swings; many analysts would place these names on the *volatile* section of their reports. And cha-ching ... volatility is incredible for stock traders. Although most on this list do not pay dividends right now, these companies are poised for higher growth. There are certainly times and situations where you could expect two to three 20–50% swings both up and down per year for the picks on this list!

These explosive stocks include NOW, YUMC, SHOP, TSLA, CELH, WWE, GDDY, NVDA, CROX, PLNT, WIX, XOM, CVX, and BA.

Companies that can monetize attention, solve problems, cure ailments, understand shifting economies, and provide fast service, ease of use, and a memorable experience should always do well.

By August 2023, I was wrapping up the trading and investing year. My company, Real Life Trading, and my portfolios survived and thrived during a pretty wild, turbulent time horizon. The stocks I'm now accumulating, that I'm aware can and probably will go lower, are SQ, SAM, ADBE, SMG, PYPL, NVDA, SHOP, PINS, TSLA, WIX, and RBLX. Knowing that my ultimate goal is to protect my investments with collars, day trading as a hedge, and slow accumulation, I aim to make a 30–40% return on each of these positions. Once I've accomplished that, if it happens, I'll look to exit and take all the earnings to reinvest into those same stocks as long-term assets or something else that seems better at the time. A quarter of the profits will go into buying three to five OTM (out of the money) LEAP (long-term equity anticipation securities) options if the long-term trend is bullish at that time.

But as discussed in Chapter 7, you always want flexibility! There are far too many sectors, industries, stocks, companies, inventions, and creations for you to be in everything or all of them. Taking the Warren Buffett approach has always worked for me! Invest in what you know, study, love, use, and understand. And when you do that, understand the money is made when you buy it! Buy it low, buy it slow, get more information on the position, and then, when everything has begun to shape up in your favor, direction, and trend, add and scale sizably. Make your profits then reinvest them into other aspects and assets of life that allow you to be cash flow positive. It's easy to make money; it's hard to keep it.

So how do I hold a winner? What movements need to occur, and how do I determine to hold past 30%?

My answer: Do I have any bills I need to pay right now?

For example, if my day trading has been banging, I've caught up on all my living expenses, and I have two to three months of reserve stacked in cash somewhere, then I can hold my swing trades or investments for longer. I hold longer in times of prosperity! But if it's been a dry spell and I need to lock in profits, I'll stop holding and cash out.

I often say, "I'll never sell the exact top," because when I sell, my brain expects the stock to free fall. When it inevitably goes higher, I feel the FOMO kick in.

In my almost two-decade trading career, I've probably placed 10,000+ trades. In seven of them, I have exited at the exact top or bottom. A few hundred have been within pennies. But, I agree, there is certainly an element where it's extremely important to know how to hold a winning stock and position.

Tips on Holding a Winner

Tip #1

If the position begins to work immediately, hold or attempt to be in the set up longer than others because it's quite rare, as pure gains often are.

How many times have you held through a retracement or pull back? You notice the trade comes back into your entry price, and you get scared.

So, when you get into a trade and *bang*, it begins to work, you never see red in your PnL, there are no pull backs, you get your full position, and it just screams! This is one of the top ten best feelings in the world, and since it brings traders so much joy, they often bail immediately because they aren't used to it. But *when* this does occur, do your best to hold. It doesn't mean you never exit, you just do your best to hold longer because you only need a few of these puppies each month or within your trading year to create an incredible financial boost.

Tip #2

You're already pretty dang profitable for the day, week, or year. You don't *need* the money or the win. You're up sizably, feeling like you're on cruise control and enjoying life. I just had a coaching student named Lera, who is a remarkable person, ask me, "How do you hold a winner?" These two above tips are exactly what I said.

Tip #3

Most of the big winners people hold are generally investments. You know the math of the Wal-Mart, Microsoft, and Apple stories. You might not have yet heard about Monster Beverages or Costco or First Solar. A friend and former coaching student has a simple investing strategy. When a stock has a valuation of less than $20 billion IPOs, he buys $1,000 of that stock when it hits the open market. And ... that's it for him.

What is his worst-case scenario? He loses $1,000 while the company and stock goes to $0, like what happened with Skillz Inc. (SKLZ) or Blue Apron Holdings, Inc. (APRN). But he wins with Shopify Inc. (SHOP), Block, Inc. (SQ), MongoDB, Inc. (MDB), and Datadog, Inc. (DDOG) where $1,000 hits a nice 20X return. It's a cool strategy that I like a lot.

The point is, if you go in *knowing* this is a long-term investment, one you've planned, thought about, and considered, it's much easier to hold.

Tip #4

I actually like this final tip as something to do in life in general. Create a time capsule for yourself, a video that you watch in the future. And, in that video, include your investment thesis with the trend along with other topics. I make one of these every year. I create a one-year, three-year, and five-year time capsule of me talking to myself about the future.

In the video, I speak to myself about my health, money, relationships, friends, family, business, dreams, and all kinds of ideas and muses. I highly encourage you to take on this practice!

And in this video you could say, "Jeremy, you just bought Unity Software at $38 per share, and you believe it will hit $100 in three years. This is not a quick cash flowing style trade, this is a core swing trade position, so hold it!"

> "Making money is more important than being correct."
> —Jeremy Alexander Newsome

Traders will hold onto their ego, their belief in the stock, their *knowingness* of what something is going to do and usually give up their profits because they held too long. While you could have easily made $3–4 per share on 500 shares and paid your car payment for the month, you *knew* AMZN was absolutely going to hit $200 and convinced yourself to hold for the next three months.

So what if AMZN did eventually hit $200? If you had to wait eight months longer than you wanted to, you didn't create any cash flow. In trading, creating an income for yourself is about repeating the math, sticking to your system, and knowing your numbers. Know your expenses, bills, income, and what to give away. When it's there, sitting in your account, take it, pay it, and move on!

The best traders in the world are those who focus on their processes while realizing it's okay to tweak, adjust, update, modify, and study them. Keep your money safe, protect it by investing it into attractive assets, and provide for your family and the world! The stock market is an incredible generator of wealth if you allow it to be while simultaneously using your money as a force for greatness!

The stock market and active trading will create greatness for you! I no longer say "good morning," I say "great morning!" because I was created in the image of greatness! I eat, breathe, drink, sleep, exude, and protrude only greatness because all I accept in my life is greatness! I expect only greatness because I am great!

Remember this each day when you wake up to know how powerful you are! Realize the universe is truly the verses you speak. The verses that you say about yourself create everything around you.

U
Ni
Verse

Universe! Be powerful. Be magnificent, and thank you for reading this book!

A NOTE FROM ME TO YOU

Dear Reader,

Embrace the journey to freedom because I know that is what you ultimately seek. You want to make the choices and decisions that spring up into your mind without asking someone else if it is okay.

The path to freedom is about clarity. You must know the exact *number* that represents financial freedom for your family, and then translate it into shares rather than dollars. Since you are a trader at heart, someone who sleeps, eats, and breathes the markets, the time is here for each part of your day to be consumed by their beautiful, organic, whimsical, and chaotic movements.

Capturing a $3 move (on any priced stock) on 1,000 shares each week equals $12,000 a month of income.

Up or down, it does not matter.

That thousand-share number tends to scare many new traders, but there are loads of stocks priced between $5 and $20 that move $3 a week both up and down. PINS, PLUG, MARA, and RIOT to name four off the top of my head.

And then when you are getting groceries and the bill is $300, you'll think, "That's $.30 on 1000 shares" or "That's 0.3R."

Become obsessed, dive all the way in, and learn how simple the game of money, wealth, and freedom is!

ABOUT THE AUTHOR

Jerremy Alexander Newsome is the founder and CEO of Real Life Trading, a stock market and wealth building education company that is one of the highest rated customer service companies on the internet. A leading global mind on stock market education, he serves on the invitation-only Forbes Business Council where he shares his insights on investment strategy, finance, and mentoring. Jeremy is a prolific investor who acutely recognizes trends and patterns in the market as evidenced by his early investments in Apple, Tesla, Ethereum, and Block.

Jeremy's mission is to transform minds and enrich lives with mentally liberating education. He knocks down barriers and creates a way for everyone to have access to the tools that have made him wealthy. Because he believes everyone should learn how to be financially free, he offers high-quality, free trading education. He even has programs for young adults and kids ages seven to fourteen. A pioneer

in "fiscal therapy," he helps others learn to master themselves—
to understand how to make the mental shift to successfully trade
without fear—and, thus, master the markets.

In addition to being one of the most highly-sought public speakers
on all things money, finance, and liquid assets, Jerremy leads retreats
that deliver massive results for people all over the world. He also
leads many masterminds and mentorships. Make sure to connect
with him to see what he is creating! His podcast, *Broke to Woke*,
ranks among the top podcasts globally, and he is the author of the #1
Amazon best-selling book *Money Grows on Trees*, as well as the first
storybook to teach young adults about the stock market, *A Stock
Market Journey: Making Sure Young Adults Win in Real Life*.

Jerremy is a lifelong philanthropist and founded the RL Foundation,
a nonprofit humanitarian organization that works to provide a
responsive and direct resource to children living in extreme poverty in
Latin America.

To learn more about Jerremy and how he uses his knowledge and
exuberance to be a force for good, visit www.jerremynewsome.com
and www.reallifetrading.com, or reach out to him on any social
media platform!

Made in the USA
Coppell, TX
13 April 2024

31255890R00089